GAINING A FOOTHOLD

Women's

Transitions

Through

Work and

College

10-03   #4129198

Commissioned by the **American
Association of University Women
Educational Foundation**

Researched by DYG Inc., and
Lake Snell Perry and Associates

Published by the
American Association of University Women Educational Foundation
1111 Sixteenth Street N.W.
Washington, DC 20036
202/728-7602
Fax: 202/872-1425
TDD: 202/785-7777
foundation@aauw.org
www.aauw.org

The AAUW Educational Foundation provides funds to advance education, research, and self-development for women and to foster equity and positive societal change.

In principle and in practice, the AAUW Educational Foundation values and supports diversity. There shall be no barriers to full participation in this organization on the basis of gender, race, creed, age, sexual orientation, national origin, or disability.

First printing: June 1999 (10M)
Cover design by Johanna White
Layout by Robert Brown Jr.

Library of Congress Catalog-in-Publication Data

Gaining a foothold : women's transitions through work and college.
        p.   cm.
    ISBN 1-879922-22-3
    1. Women—Education (Higher)—United States Case studies.
  2. School-to-work transition—United States Case studies.
  I. American Associaion of University Women. Educational
  Foundation.
  LC1756.G35   1999
  378.1'9822—dc21

                                                            99-15622
                                                     CIP

Table of Contents

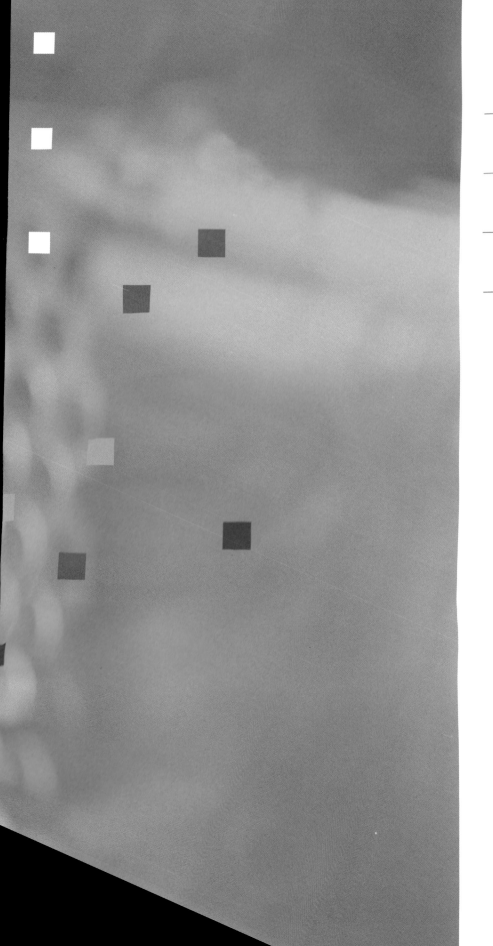

Introduction

THE RESEARCH CONTEXT

■

If experts are correct, higher education institutions—and their students—may look radically different in the 21st century. Consider the following:

■ At his inauguration as The Johns Hopkins University president, William Brody predicted that "we will witness the transformation of the university from a physical campus, or specific geographic location, to a dispersed, virtual campus." He urged that "we must view the educational process not as a finite encounter lasting a few semesters, but as a lifelong continuum." A U.S. Department of Education report concurs with some of Brody's vision. It speculates that postsecondary education will increasingly be delivered in "module" form— distributed throughout a person's life—rather than in the discrete package of a four-year bachelor's degree.

■ Chancellor Donald Langenberg of the University of Maryland also imagines "virtual universities," where learning will occur "wherever students can connect to the World Wide Web. Students will be able to move easily among educational institutions," he speculates, "perhaps enrolling at several real and/or virtual universities, or perhaps studying one subject at the high school level and other subjects with college professors." A universal "college-credit banking system will have to evolve." Students will "demonstrate their mastery of certain skills at different points in their lives and will receive certificates of achievement" that will contribute to a performance portfolio.

■ A former University of Michigan president imagines 21st-century higher education as a "knowledge industry" characterized by a "shift in focus from faculty members and their specialties to the needs of all kinds of students at various points in their lives."

■ Finally, even high school graduates sense shifts on the higher education landscape. Research based on a series of national forums with honors students reveals a broad belief that higher education "does not necessarily mean a four-year college or university education." Students agree that they can "profit from many kinds of higher education institutions," including technical colleges, and that college education, in any case, should be "for a lifetime."[1]

These visions of higher education in the next century share a conviction that both education and the definition of the "student" are becoming more fluid and flexible. People are making educational decisions throughout their lives, rather than limiting their choice to whether or not to go to a four-year college immediately after high school.

Second, they recognize that higher education's infrastructure is changing and may need to change further to accommodate more diverse students, not only by race and ethnicity, but by age and learning needs. Students over age 40 represent the fastest-growing age group in postsecondary education, yet only 27 percent of students in this group receive financial aid for returning to school. Older students are more likely to work full-time, study part-time, and have family commitments. Higher education institutions often do not match the needs of this growing population of students, who are eager to go back to school and to combine work with formal education. Even among young students, there has been "a substantial increase" in the numbers who combine work and education, according to The National Center for Postsecondary Improvement. Between 1984 and 1994, the proportion of students engaging simultaneously in college and work increased by nearly eight percent.[2] Additionally, more students who move directly from high school to college are taking longer than the traditional four years to complete their bachelor's degrees.

Visions of the 21st-century university also recognize that economic and technological changes invite, and perhaps demand, more interaction among education, school, and work. The popular idea of "lifelong learning," with people developing their knowledge, skills, and interests throughout their lives, is in part driven by economic and technological changes that require the frequent updating of skills. Additionally, the workplace has changed from offering cradle-to-grave job security to a more fluid (or volatile) economy characterized by downsizing, outsourcing, "task employment," temporary work, self-employment, and rapid technological change. This new context of work will probably stimulate more interaction between educational and occupational worlds in the future. "School to Work" programs in the 1990s, for example, which combine high school coursework with internships and apprenticeships, have already intermeshed the classroom and work settings as dual sites for learning. In this new economy, women can realistically expect to make more transitions—by choice or necessity—between their career or job and their education.

Women, specifically, may also find that their need for education changes as their lives take different turns— from a welfare mother struggling to get off public assistance to a mid-level manager attempting to break through the glass ceiling; from a woman graduating from college and beginning her career to one returning to school in order to reenter the job market after raising children. If women are to be equipped to face these changes, we need to know more about how, when, and why education affects these transitions, the barriers women face, and the effects of education on their careers and lives.

Goals of the Report

■

In light of these changes in higher education and the economy, this research explores how and why women make educational transitions. It focuses on the factors that influence women as they move from high school to work, from high school to college, and from the workforce back to school.

The AAUW Educational Foundation's overall goals in this research are to:

■ Explore the institutional factors that affect women's decisions at different transition points

■ Compare men's and women's experiences of transitions

■ Understand the complex interaction of personal, social, cultural, economic, and institutional variables that influence how, when, and why educational transitions occur

■ Understand how women make decisions about schooling and education

■ Clarify how institutions create obstacles or opportunities for women making educational transitions

Study Methodology

Qualitative Phase

Lake Snell Perry and Associates conducted focus groups in September and October 1998. Areas of inquiry included challenges, opportunities, motivations, expectations, and goals for the future; decision-making processes; institutional obstacles, barriers, or incentives to pursue postsecondary education; sources of information; views on two-year versus four-year schools; and a retrospective examination of participants' own educational and career choices.

This research phase consisted of 10 focus groups: in Atlanta, one group of white boys ages 16–19 and one racially mixed group of women, ages 20–30, both groups transitioning from school to work; in Los Angeles, one group of young Latinas, ages 16–19, and one group of minority women, both groups with experience at a two-year institution or community college; in Altoona (PA), one group of white women with educational experiences similar to their counterparts in Los Angeles, and one group of lower-income white women who went to work before continuing their education; in Baltimore, one group of white girls, ages 16–19, and one group of African American girls in the same age group; and, finally, in Chicago, one group of African American women who worked before returning to school, and one group of upper-income white women who followed a similar pattern.

Because of the limited number of respondents and the restrictions of recruiting, this research phase must be considered in a qualitative frame of reference. This phase of the study cannot be considered reliable or valid in the statistical sense. It is intended to provide insight, knowledge, and opinions about issues and concerns to help enrich and shape the quantitative phase of the research, which does provide statistically valid information.

Quantitative Phase

In December 1998 and January 1999, DYG, Inc., conducted a national telephone survey of 1,070 respondents undergoing one of the following three transitions: high school to college, high school to full-time work, and work back to postsecondary education.* Each transition was defined as follows:

- Transition Group #1: High School to College. These respondents, identified as "School to College" in this report, met the following criteria:
  - Graduated from high school in the past three years
  - Went directly to an accredited higher education program (a two-year or four-year college, full- or part-time)
  - Did not work full-time before college (summer jobs the exception); do not work full-time while in college

DYG, Inc., conducted 317 interviews with this group (212 women, 105 men).

---

* Some of the respondents may have recently completed a transition.

- Transition Group #2: Work to College. These respondents, identified as "Work to College," met the following criteria:
  - Worked full-time for at least a year after high school and before attending college or graduate school
  - Currently enrolled full-time in a postsecondary degree program (a two-year, four-year, or a graduate/professional program)
  - Can still be working part-time or full-time while in school

DYG, Inc., conducted 453 interviews with this group (345 women, 108 men).

- Transition Group #3: High School to Work. These respondents, identified as "School to Work," met the following criteria:
  - Graduated from high school in the past several years
  - Did not go on to college
  - Work at least 20 hours per week

DYG, Inc., conducted 300 interviews with this group (200 women, 100 men).[3]

All statistically significant differences cited in the report are reliable with a 5 percent margin of error.

Executive

Summary

KEY FINDINGS AND CONCLUSIONS

■

AAUW Educational Foundation commissioned *Gaining a Foothold: Women's Transitions Through Work and College* to learn more about the differences and similarities among distinct groups of students making education-related transitions. As a Foundation that produces research on the themes of gender, equity, and education, we had a particular interest in understanding how men and women navigate educational transitions.

One crucial, overall finding of *Gaining a Foothold* is that "students" are a far more heterogeneous population than that of 18-year-olds who pack their bags and leave for college immediately after high school graduation. While others have spoken of the "track" or pipeline from high school to college, this report uses the metaphor of a "spiral" to denote, among other things, the continuing role of education over a woman's lifetime as she moves in and out of postsecondary education. Many students—by choice or necessity—follow a circuitous path through postsecondary education rather than a straight line from high school, to college, to graduate or professional school, to career. The diversity of the student population by age, race, ethnicity, socioeconomic status, academic preparedness, and educational interests and needs will become only more pronounced as the next century progresses.

In light of these changes, institutions, educators, researchers, policymakers, counselors, K–12 teachers,

and individuals can benefit from rethinking crucial educational concepts such as access, social equity, and institutional services and design.

This research describes three groups of students and prospective students—those moving from high school to full-time work ("School to Work"), those moving from high school to college ("School to College"), and those moving from full-time work back to college* ("Work to College"). It explores how and why women and men make educational decisions; the institutional obstacles and opportunities they face; the interaction of education and other life changes such as marriage, divorce, and parenthood; and their views of how colleges might be more responsive and accessible to a broader range of students. The report is designed to help reconceptualize the identity and needs of the "student," and to help K–16 institutions meet the needs of these specific populations, by contributing a new dimension to the body of research on educational transitions.

Choices and Chances: The Decision-Making Process

Significantly more women than men who moved from high school to the full-time work force report that not attending college was a decision based on circumstances or "forces beyond [their] control."

---

* We use the term "college" for continuity; however, students returning from work to college, or students combining full-time work and at least 20 hours a week of college, may be pursuing completion of a bachelor's degree, a two-year associate's degree, a certificate, or a postgraduate degree. "College" encompasses each of these elements of postsecondary education.

Fewer women than men respond that the decision was "basically their own choice."

- Male high school graduates who moved into the work force were significantly more likely than their female counterparts to:
  - cite a lack of interest in college and a belief that they could "get a decent job" without college as "very important" factors in their decision
  - describe their employment as a "career" rather than "just a job"
  - have never seriously considered going to college in the first place.

- Conversely, a significantly higher percentage of School to College men report that they "feel like [they] got pushed into college by other people" and "never really made the decision [themselves]" (17% of men to 8% of women).

Goals and Aspirations

Women have a dual agenda for attending college. Whether going to college straight from high school or after working for some time, they attend college for both economic (career, income) and self-fulfillment (personal enrichment) reasons. Women in all college-bound groups place more emphasis on self-fulfillment than do men.

- There is a misperception that nontraditional students return to school to learn specific skills to further their careers. This overlooks the desire for personal enrichment and general intellectual development that is an especially pronounced goal for women across the transition groups.
  - Nine out of 10 School to College and Work to College women judge pursuing "a career that is interesting and personally fulfilling" to be a "very important" reason for attending college.

Almost eight out of 10 women in both groups—and significantly more women than men in the School to College group—choose "personal enrichment" as a very important goal. Obtaining a better-paying or a well-paying job is judged a very important goal by seven out of 10 and almost eight out of 10 Work to College and School to College women, respectively.

- Women returning to school, especially, emphasize quality-of-career issues in focus group conversations. They seek jobs that have inherent value and meaning and for which they receive not only financial compensation—which is important—but work flexibility, autonomy, and satisfaction.

- Younger students going straight to college from high school are more likely to see a college diploma as a necessary credential than older, returning students.
  - Sixty percent of School to College women and men say getting "the piece of paper" or a necessary credential is a very important goal, in contrast to 38 percent of Work to College students.

- There are more significant differences in goals for college by sex among School to College students than among Work to College students.

Obstacles and Barriers

Money Matters

Money is cited as the most significant obstacle for both men and women contemplating higher education. Over one-half of the School to College group and about two-thirds of each of the other two groups say that "a lack of money and/or financial aid" was an obstacle to going to college. In some cases, however, money affects men and women differently:

- Women moving from high school to work are significantly more likely than men in that group to say that a lack of money is a barrier to education (69% to 55%) and that college is too expensive for them (71% to 58%).

- School to Work women are also significantly more likely than men to feel that better information about financial aid would have made them "much more likely" to go to college (51% to 33%).

- Women are significantly more likely than men (32% to 19% in the Work to College population) to say that **credit card debt** was a barrier to going to college.
  - People of color, in comparison to whites, are more likely to say that credit card debt poses an educational barrier (41% to 26% in the Work to College group).
  - The problem of credit card debt begins as early as high school and is more pronounced for women than men. Fully one in five School to Work respondents cite credit card debt as an obstacle to college.

Academic and Test Performance Anxieties: The Story of Self-Fulfilling Prophecies?

Anxiety impedes some from attending college. The source of anxiety most often cited as an obstacle to attending college is "nervousness about the academic requirements," mentioned by almost half of the School to College group and by 36 percent of the School to Work group.

- Approximately one-quarter to one-third of women in each of the three groups say that anxiety about SAT scores is an obstacle to college.

- Among the School to College students, women are significantly more likely than men to cite SAT scores as an obstacle (34% to 22%).
- More people of color than whites who did not attend college immediately after high school feel that doing away with standardized tests would have made them "much more likely" to go to college (37% to 20%).

It is important to note that these students were impeded from applying to college by **anxieties** about low scores, not by low scores themselves.

- Significantly more School to Work men than women (20% to 9%) cite their feeling that "it was too difficult to get accepted" as a "very important" obstacle to college.
  - People of color and students from families with incomes under $40,000 are also significantly more likely to be deterred from college by a feeling that it would be too difficult to get accepted.

Skepticism About SAT Fairness and Accuracy

- College-bound students do not perceive the SAT to be an accurate predictor of academic performance. Only 15 percent of School to College women and 25 percent of School to College men judge them to be accurate gauges of future college performance.

- Roughly half of the women in the two college-bound groups feel that students who can afford SAT preparation classes have an unfair advantage, and between one-third and half of the women in these groups feel that the SAT is a fair and unbiased measure of ability. Only slightly more college-bound men—roughly one in four—feel that the SAT is a fair and unbiased measure of ability.

Treatment of Women and Minorities in College

- On the whole, women in all three transition groups perceive college to be an inviting place for them. Only about one-fifth of women in the two college-bound groups agree that the "treatment of women in higher education" or "society's attitude toward women" creates an obstacle to college.

- School to Work women who did not go to college do not feel that college is a "tougher place for women" (only 16% say college is tougher for women). Men's and women's opinions are similar on the issue, with 18 percent of men agreeing that college is tougher for women than men.

- College appears somewhat less inviting for people of color, roughly one-third of whom in the college-bound groups agree that the "treatment of racial and ethnic minorities in higher education" poses an obstacle for them.

Guidance Counselors: A Missed Opportunity?

Over half of all three groups (57% of the School to Work group, 59% of the School to College group, and 62% of the Work to College group) report being somewhat satisfied or not satisfied at all with their guidance counselor experience.

- Students who report having average or below average grades are especially likely to feel that their "guidance counselors did not give [them] enough time or attention."

- In focus group conversations, participants felt that counselors sometimes determined whether or not a student was "college material," and focused on what they could not do immediately following graduation instead of providing more concrete,

long-term guidance about how the student might eventually achieve a stated goal.

The Information Gap: What They Don't Know Hurts Them

There is a strong consensus that students would benefit from more information about the college application and selection process. Fully 72 percent of the School to Work group, for example, speculate that better information about colleges, degrees, and programs would have made them more likely to attend college.

- Across all three transition points, women are significantly more likely than men to agree that better information would have influenced their decision. One in three School to Work men feels that more information would have had "no effect at all" on their decision, in contrast to only one in five women.

- When it comes to getting information, nothing succeeds like success: Students across all three transition points who report having received above average SAT scores and above average grades are significantly more likely to report that they "knew a lot" about the college selection process.

- Income affects students' perceptions of how much information they received. Almost all of the School to College respondents (94%) who report family incomes under $50,000 feel that they needed "much more information," in contrast to 80 percent of those with family incomes over $50,000.

- Information about careers is even harder to come by than information about college. About one-third of both the School to Work and School to

College group agree that it was difficult to get information about careers. Twenty percent of the School to College set, in contrast, feel it was difficult to get information about college.

■ Women are more eclectic in their decisionmaking than men, reporting that a wider variety of sources of information, ranging from campus visits to books, were "very influential" in their thinking.

■ Students who report knowing a lot about college are more likely to attend a four-year school, while those who do not are more likely to attend a two-year school.

Life Stages/Educational Transitions

Age Is More Often Cited as an Obstacle by Returning Women than Men

■ Although adult students now account for nearly half of college enrollments overall, significantly more women than men feel that their age posed a barrier to college. Of those Work to College women who said they were older than their fellow students, 18 percent cite age as an obstacle, compared with only three percent of their male counterparts.

Spouses Appear as Obstacles or as Irrelevant to the Educational Transition

■ Twenty-one percent of the married Work to College students report that "lack of spouse support" was a "significant obstacle." In another question, 32 percent respond that being married had "no effect" on their decision to go back to school.

The Paradox of Children

■ Seventy-five percent of the School to Work group (men and women) who were pregnant or caring for children at the time they graduated from high school report that "having to care for children" was a very important reason they did not go to college. A vast majority—82 percent—name it as the "single most important" reason for not seeking postsecondary education.

■ Although parents seeking further education may often face institutional barriers and obstacles, children also emerged in focus group research as powerful motivators and incentives for women to return to or continue school.

■ Students with children need more **time and flexibility.** The highest percentage of the School to Work group (28%) choose "more financial aid for anyone who needs it" as the single most important thing that would have influenced their transition. However, among those with children, the highest percentage—26 percent—choose "more flexible scheduling of classes to accommodate outside demands," and the second-highest percentage (19%) choose colleges offering day care services. Another 19 percent choose "more financial aid" as the single most important factor.

■ Work to College students with children face a broader range of obstacles than their counterparts without children. Obstacles they deemed to be "significant" included credit card debt, nervousness about academic requirements, lack of motivation or desire, low grades in high school, anxiety about SAT scores, society's attitude toward women in general, treatment of women in higher education, and a spouse's or partner's lack of support.

- Work to College parents also differ in their judgment that the "treatment of women in higher education" constitutes a significant obstacle (13% of respondents with children in comparison to 5% of respondents without children).
- School to Work parents are significantly more likely than their childless peers to receive little or no encouragement for education from their friends and spouses, and are more likely to report that parents and teachers were "not an influence at all" in their transition.

Perceptions of Education, Economy, and Careers

The Future Job Market

- Roughly two-thirds of the Work to College and School to College groups say that they did consider economic projections and the future job market when they made their educational decision. The ratio is reversed, however, in the School to Work group, where 63 percent report that the economy did not influence their decision or transition.

Although high school students bound for college feel that they have considered economic realities in their decision, other research shows that college-bound students—both men and women—dramatically overestimate their chances of getting professional jobs, for example, and express little interest in the career areas likely to grow in the next century.

Computers "Take Over"

- All respondents—from both sexes, all ages, races, and ethnicities, and across all transition points—firmly believe that computers are, in a high school woman's words, "taking over the world."
- Fully 85 percent of the Work to College and 78 percent of the School to College groups agree that "it is almost impossible to get a decent job today without a firm knowledge of computers." Seventy percent of the School to Work group feel that computer skills are "very important" to getting a good job today.

The High Educational Bar

Almost unanimously, respondents undergoing any transition, and from all social backgrounds, feel that a high school degree is essential for getting a good job. Substantial numbers now report that a college degree is the minimum prerequisite for career success.

- Roughly one-third of the two college-bound groups believe a college degree is "essential" for a good job. Between 94 percent and 96 percent agree that "in the future, it will be even harder to get a decent job without a college degree."

- Views of the college degree and formal education are somewhat ambivalent, however. Although respondents place great value on high school diplomas and, to a lesser extent, college degrees, larger percentages of respondents in all three transition groups rate "having people skills," "real world work experience," "interviewing well," and "critical thinking skills" as essential for a good job. Forty percent of the School to Work group believe that "you don't really need to go to college today to get a decent job."

- People of color agree that a postgraduate degree is an "important" factor significantly more often than whites. They cite the degree as "essential" almost twice as often as white respondents across all three transition groups.

Solutions: Making College More Accessible and Equitable

Community Colleges Rate Highly as Role Models of Institutional Flexibility, Affordability, and Parent-Friendly Campuses

- Most students, including those in four-year colleges and universities, judge community colleges quite positively. Not unexpectedly, the most favorable ratings of community colleges come from the Work to College group and students with children.
  - Seventy-five percent of the Work to College group agree that community colleges offer a better deal financially than four-year colleges.
  - Eighty-three percent of Work to College students enrolled in two-year schools agree that community colleges are better for students with children. A majority—65 percent—of the Work to College students in four-year schools also agree with the statement.

- Parents in the Work to College group are significantly more likely than those without children to agree that community colleges are better for:
  - Students who work
  - Getting personal attention from faculty
  - First-generation college students
  - Convenience
  - Flexibility in scheduling

Money Matters

- "More financial aid for anyone who needs it" was the item most often favored by women to make college more accessible, significantly more than men in two groups. Each of the transition groups also cite tax incentives to make it easier for people to continue their education as one of their top three recommendations. Across all three groups, two-thirds to over three-quarters of women favor more financial aid and tax incentives.

Better Sources of Information Needed about Financial Aid

- Significantly more women than men across all three transition points strongly favor better sources of information about financial aid as an improvement that would make going to college easier. Fully 80 percent of School to Work women, compared with 66 percent of School to Work men, favor better sources of information, which would include more user-friendly, accessible, and streamlined financial aid information.

More Information about College and Careers— and More Tangible Information

- Women students, especially, prefer tangible— human, face-to-face—sources of information, and all students feel that they would have benefited from more career and college information as they considered their decision.

Employer Incentives: Rare but Highly Effective

- Employers and co-workers lent encouragement to very few employees in either the Work to College or the School to Work groups. Only about two in 10 say they were strongly encouraged by someone at their workplace to return to school. Nor do employers typically offer financial incentives for employees to pursue college. Yet those Work to College group who did receive financial incentives overwhelmingly reported (75%) that it was an important factor in their return to school.

Day Care Services

- Seventy-four percent of the Work to College parents say more "day care and schedules to accommodate students with children" is a "large help" in returning to school, and almost all assess it as at least somewhat of a help.

- Seventy-four percent of School to Work parents say that day care services would make them "much more likely" to attend college.

Returning Students Favor Institutional Flexibility

- Women returning to school are significantly more likely than men to value more flexible scheduling of classes (69% to 53%) and more flexibility regarding the length of time needed to complete different programs (55% to 40%). Evidently, women returning to school feel especially stretched for time and imagine that they would benefit more from flexible schedules and timetables.

Profiles

of

Transitions

WHO TRANSITIONS FROM SCHOOL TO COLLEGE?

■

"Tara" is an African American 11th grader from Baltimore who plans to move directly from high school to college. She is involved in hospital volunteer activities, lacrosse, and cheerleading. When asked to "draw a map" of her future, Tara paces it around a series of academic milestones. "Now," she writes, "I am pulling out [my] hair, finding scholarships and applying to schools." She writes that she will "attend a four-year college, most likely in Maryland. Try to excel at college. Attend medical school, focusing on pediatrics and sports medicine. Graduate from Med School and complete a residency" before starting her own practice. She imagines "marriage, kids, and tak[ing] care of her mother and business" as transitions made after her education and career preparation. After she retires, she speculates that she might like to "work in an aquarium and travel."

Background Characteristics

School to College students report in this survey that they were especially successful in high school: eight in 10 say they had "above average" grades, and only one in 100 reports "below average" grades. Roughly half feel that their SAT scores were "above average," with 36 percent reporting at least "average" scores.

The School to College transition students are likely to have parents with post-high school education. Half (50%) of the School to College students' mothers and 60 percent of the fathers have at least a college degree, with roughly a quarter of the students reporting that their mothers or fathers have a high school degree or less. These students have also enjoyed relative affluence: almost half (46%) estimate their family's annual income at $50,000 or more.

Educational Characteristics

The overwhelming majority (92%) of women and men transitioning directly from high school to college report that they are attending four-year colleges or universities. Sixty-seven percent (67%) are attending public universities or colleges, and 33 percent are attending private institutions. The School to College transition student is most likely seeking a bachelor's degree, although four percent are targeting an associate's degree. School to College respondents are optimistic that they can complete their targeted degree in four to under five years (45%) or even in three to under four years (22%). However, 16 percent do anticipate a longer time to completion, ranging from five to six years or more.

There are no differences by sex in terms of degrees sought or types of institutions attended. There are differences by sex in course of study and major. School to College students report a wide array of majors, none of which garners more than nine percent of the overall responses. However, 20 percent of men—significantly more than the five percent of women—record their major as engineering and applied sciences, although the major accounts for only nine percent of the overall responses. Men are also significantly more likely than women to declare technology management and operations as a major (9% of men, 3% of women). Physics and earth sciences (4% of men, no women), economics (4% of men, 1% of women), public policy (3% of men, no women) and, among the humanities disciplines, history (5% of men, no women), all attract more men than women, although they are less popular majors overall.

In addition to their strong representation in the humanities and social sciences, School to College women in this survey predominate in several traditionally "male" college majors, including the Medicine or "pre-med" major (9% of women, 3% of men), chemistry and chemical biology (3% of women, no men) and, interestingly, a cluster of Business and Management-related majors, including an MBA program, marketing, business and government, international economy, general management, human resources and labor, and service management (19% of women total, 6% of men total).

Men and women enroll equally in several curricular areas, including most notably, psychology, education, and the biological sciences.

Personal Characteristics

The typical School to College student is unencumbered by family or parental responsibilities. Almost nine out of 10 report being single and living with their family (when not away at school), and 10 percent report being single and living alone. Only one percent was married or raising a child when they moved into college. Almost half—46 percent—of the School to College segment combine some part-time work with college.

WHO TRANSITIONS FROM SCHOOL TO WORK?

"Mary" is a 17-year-old Latina from Los Angeles, in her last year of high school, who will move directly into full-time work after graduation. She has plotted a possible future for herself. She may join the Marines and train to be a helicopter pilot. Then, after four or five years, she envisions enrolling in college, and later, after 10 years or so, "getting married and having children." In focus group conversation, she describes her life as "really busy. I mostly worry about my grades, just keeping up with everything. I have priorities and I want to have fun, but I have to do my school work and I have to do sports ... I want a car. So these are all issues that I have to deal with." When asked to give advice to an imaginary future daughter, "Mary" writes, "I want you to do what makes you happy. I don't care if you like working at Taco Bell. I would, though, love to see you become a successful woman and have no regrets about your decisions."

Background Characteristics

The School to Work transition students present an almost opposite image of the School to College students in terms of reported academic and family background.

Few School to Work students appraise their grades or their SAT scores as "above average" (29% and 16%, respectively), with the majority placing their academic performance in the "average" category.

The School to Work students are most likely to have parents without a college degree. Whereas half of the School to College students report that their mothers received a college degree or more, over half (55%) of the School to Work respondents report that their

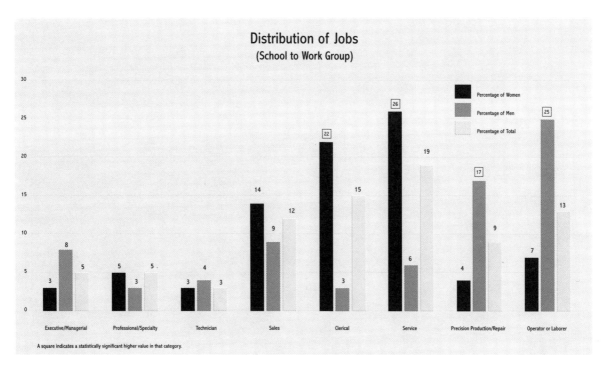

Distribution of Jobs
(School to Work Group)

Percentage of Women
Percentage of Men
Percentage of Total

A square indicates a statistically significant higher value in that category.

mothers received a high school degree or less. Half (52%) report that their fathers received a high school degree or less. Eighteen percent (18%) and 15 percent—fewer than one in five—report that their fathers or mothers, respectively, completed college or postgraduate education. Almost eight out of 10 (79%) of the School to Work students estimate their family's annual income at the time they graduated from high school to be below $50,000.

Job Characteristics

School to Work men and women cluster, along stark lines, in careers "traditional" for their sex. The highest percentages of School to Work women are in clerical or secretarial jobs (22% of women, 3% of men) and service-oriented jobs such as food preparation, hairdressing, janitorial services, and housekeeping (26% of women, 6% of men). A smaller percentage of women (14%) are in sales, compared with nine percent of men. The highest percentage of men (25%, 7% of women), in contrast, cluster in the job categories of operator, fabricator or laborer (an assembler or machine operator, for example), and the second highest percentage (17% of men, 4% of women) report that they work in the fields of crafts or precision production or repair (auto mechanics, for example).

Personal Characteristics

School to Work respondents are much more likely than their School to College counterparts to have family responsibilities when they transition out of high school. Whereas only one in 100 of the School to College segment reports being responsible for a child at the time of transition, 15 percent, or roughly one in seven, of the School to Work respondents had child care responsibilities as they transitioned out of high school. Fourteen percent (14%) of the School to Work segment also report having been older than other students at the time of high school graduation.

WHO TRANSITIONS FROM WORK TO COLLEGE?

■

"The choices you make in your life will be your own," "Melissa" advises her imaginary daughter. "Live life, discover, and find all the opportunities that you have. Always educate yourself.... Don't forget your dreams, for [they are] part of you." Melissa, a white 28-year-old who recently completed college after working out of high school, lives in Altoona, Pennsylvania. In focus group conversation, she describes herself as "divorced with two girls.... I worked over the summer, but then I took time off to take care of my grandfather. Now I'm looking for work." Melissa wanted to return to school, she says, because she "didn't like what I was doing. I was working weird hours, and I had two little girls, and I wanted a normal life."*

Background Characteristics

Mirroring the School to College pattern, the Work to College student is likely to report having received "above average" grades and SAT scores (70% and 48%, respectively) while in high school. Also like her School to College counterpart, the Work to College student is likely to have a college-educated parent. Nearly half of both the Work to College mothers and fathers (46% and 48%, respectively) possess at least a college degree.

Eighty-one percent (81%) of the Work to School students report household incomes of under $50,000 *at the time of their transition.*

Educational and Occupational Characteristics

One in four Work to School students is seeking a bachelor's degree or less, and almost three in four are seeking a postgraduate degree such as a master's, a professional degree, or a doctorate. The vast majority (88%) attend a public university. Most attend a four-year university (76%), although 16 percent attend a two-year college or a technical or vocational school.

Some of the divisions by sex evident in School to College students' selection of majors appear in the Work to College segment as well. The single largest percentage of women in this cohort (17% of women, 9% of men) say that they are majoring in education and teaching fields, a significantly higher percentage than in the male cohort. The second highest percentage of women (10%) are pursuing the medical sciences. Significantly more male Work to College students than female students are pursuing degrees in engineering (7% of men, 1% of women), history (4% of men, 1% of women), technology operations (8% of men, 2% of women), or mathematics (3% of men, no women).

The largest percentage of Work to School respondents (30%) say they work the same number of hours as they did before they went back to school, with women more likely to report this than men. More men than women say they work fewer hours or no longer work at all now that they attend school (37% overall work fewer hours, and 22% overall no longer work at all).

Personal Characteristics

The Work to College segment—typically older than the other segments in the survey—also resembles the School to Work segment in the percentage with family and personal responsibilities at the time of transition. Thirteen percent were responsible for a child (in comparison to 15% of School to Work students) when they returned to school, and 20 percent were married.

Decision Making in Context

THE TWO SPIRALS

◼

A theme running through this study is that of two spirals. Many of the individual factors that will be discussed interact to produce either a spiral that moves high school students directly toward college, or a spiral that pulls students away from college out of high school.

In contrast to "tracking," which refers mostly to the formal mechanisms within schools that sort students according to perceived abilities, the metaphor of a spiral captures the interaction of educational, familial, and social factors that cumulatively affect the decisions high school students make.

Additionally, the spiral connotes the ongoing nature of educational transitions for many individuals throughout their lives: As the National Center for Postsecondary Improvement describes, the pipeline from high school to "going away to college" to graduate and professional school may still apply for many middle- or upper-income students, but other students, by choice or necessity, are increasingly following "different patterns through their education careers, swirling in and out of a variety of educational institutions at different times in their lives," and facing, in effect, a spiral of educational transitions.

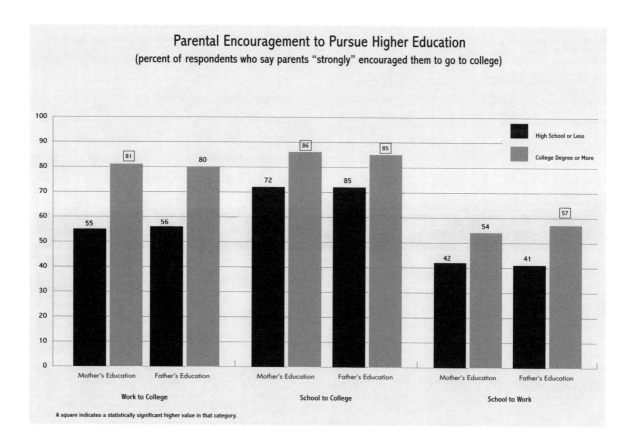

Parental Encouragement to Pursue Higher Education
(percent of respondents who say parents "strongly" encouraged them to go to college)

A square indicates a statistically significant higher value in that category.

"Generational College": The Spiral Toward Higher Education

According to this survey, the parents of the children in this spiral are more likely to have been to college themselves and are more likely to have a higher income, which enables them to finance more easily their children's pursuit of college. As shown in the following tables, these parents are also more likely to stress the importance of higher education, encourage their children to attain a college degree, and possess the needed "cultural capital" of deeper knowledge of and more information about higher education.

Focus group participants keenly and vividly described the "spiral toward" college. Many of them saw college as an assumption—a pro forma post-high school transition. "Normal people go to high school, and then they go to college, and then they get a job," a Baltimore high school graduate notes. "That's what society says. It expects you to go to high school and go to college and then get a job and have kids." Perceiving it as a "normal" sequencing of events, several high school students on the cusp of college or full-time work did not experience the college transition as a decision point but rather as an inevitable next step. As a Los Angeles woman clarifies, "I guess the only choice I saw was college, and that was it, but that is not all there is … . It's kind of like, you have to go to school. There wasn't an option, or nothing else was discussed." A Latina high school senior similarly explains, "With the grammar school I went to, you knew you were going to a private high school and then you know you are going to college right after it. You wouldn't even have the choice."

Others pinpoint family expectations as a primary motivator to attend college, one labeling the phenomenon "generational college." Those with parents who did not go to college, this Chicagoan says, "are kind of at a disadvantage … . My friend was [the] fifth generation to go to [the University of] Georgia … . When you've got that kind of thing … you almost don't want to let your family down. But when you've got [people] like my family … it's not going to disappoint my dad if I don't go to college. So I think that's kind of a disadvantage that people [like me] have."

Participants in the focus groups with and without college-educated parents agree that this parental influence runs deep and begins early, a few commenting that children "are groomed from the time they came out of the womb" by parents who "start saving the month that they [are] born … I mean, it's just ingrained in them, so there [is] never any question." In contrast, an African American woman recalls of her community, "We were groomed the way our parents knew how. And it was basically survival."

The Effect of Income on Grades and SAT Scores (School to College Group)	Family Income	
	Less than $50,000	$50,000 or more
Percent who report "above average" grades	75	86
Percent who report "above average" SAT scores	42	56

A square indicates a statistically significant higher value in that category.

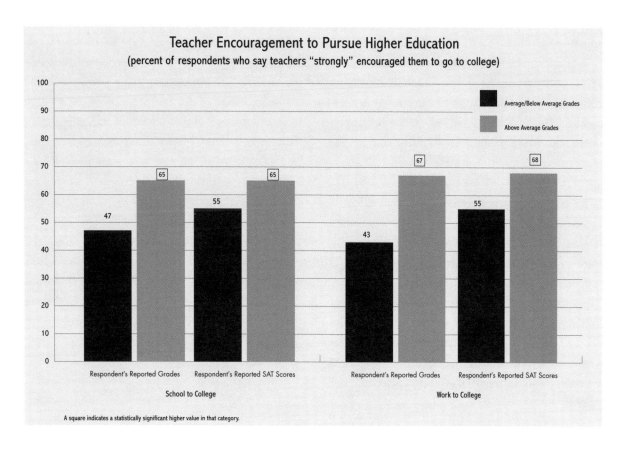

Teacher Encouragement to Pursue Higher Education
(percent of respondents who say teachers "strongly" encouraged them to go to college)

A square indicates a statistically significant higher value in that category.

School to College respondents who reported a family income of $50,000 or above are significantly more likely than those with $50,000 or below to report "above-average" grades and SAT scores.

In turn, higher grades, early high school tracking into honors and advanced courses, and SAT scores increase the likelihood of these children receiving encouragement from teachers and guidance counselors to go to college.

One college-bound high school senior in a Baltimore focus group recalls school, for example, as a place where "you have to do well. Everybody expects you to do well." Another explains, "I just figured I would take my SATs and I'd just go to college. And they would offer me scholarships and things like that."

Cumulatively, as they reinforce one another, these factors make attending college directly out of high

school more likely. It bears emphasis that high SAT scores and above-average grades in high school are the endgame in a spiral toward college that, as focus group participants intuitively realize, begins earlier in life. Other researchers argue that by eighth grade or even grade school, "the die is cast" and it may be too late to remedy inadequate academic preparation in reading, math, and science, or to compensate for social and economic inequities among students.[4]

"It Wasn't Something that Was Pushed": The Spiral Away From Higher Education

Many of the same factors at work in the spiral toward college function in reverse to push students away from college after high school. According to the survey, parents of children in this spiral are likely never to have attended college and are less likely to have the financial resources for their children's education (both the actual expenses of attending college and money for learning about colleges and the application process) or a knowledge about higher education and information about the transition process. They are also less likely to impress upon their children the importance of college and are less likely to express positive attitudes toward college.

In focus group conversations, the maternal influence appeared especially strong for women, as they referred to their mother's educational attainment more frequently than to their father's. This trend is supported by survey research: female School to Work respondents in the survey are significantly more likely than their male counterparts to have a mother who did not receive a postsecondary education (60% of women to 47% of men). However, equal numbers of men and women report that their father did not

> **"**
> *I wish I had those three ghosts from 'A Christmas Carol' or something, to show me what would happen if I would have done this … . To be able to look into the future … . That would have affected my decision a whole lot.* **"**
>
> —Baltimore, white, first-year college student

complete college. Research in 1998 similarly found that 39% of high-achieving high school students, both male and female, cited their mothers as the "greatest influence in their lives."[5] "My mom wasn't educated," an Atlanta woman recalls, "so she didn't know how to help me go to find out about education." When "my mom was growing up," a

Baltimorean similarly explains, "a lot of her friends didn't go, so she didn't go. It wasn't something that was pushed." It is interesting that a few respondents whose mothers or fathers did not attend college lamented the lack of information about college more than the lack of money for college. As one comments, "My mother had all three of us, and she didn't have a penny, so she didn't really know *information* to tell me about college."

These parental and familial factors may reduce the chances that children will perform well in school as manifested in high school grades and SAT scores. Lower grades and SAT scores reduce the likelihood that children will receive information or encouragement from teachers and guidance counselors to go to college.

Students with family responsibilities—those who become pregnant, are responsible for the care of someone else, or get married before graduating from high school—are less likely to go to college.

All of these factors function to make attending college less likely for these young men and women.

Dissatisfaction with Both Spirals

Not surprisingly, students whose parents lacked the wherewithal to "push" them toward college or to provide information about college expressed some dissatisfaction with (or at least resignation to) the disadvantages they faced in making the transition out of high school.

Somewhat more surprising is the dissatisfaction among students with the positive "spiral toward" college. In focus group conversations, a few recent or soon-to-be high school graduates, for example, distinguished between receiving "information" about education and being "pushed" or "forced" into a decision that they had not fully embraced or chosen themselves. "They're not really giving you information," a Baltimorean clarifies, "they're just saying you need to go to college. College is the way to live your life. That's all they say. They don't give out 'information.'" They "think they're helping you," a high school student elaborates, "but really they're putting all this pressure on you."

Other students on the spiral toward college after high school used a language of force to describe the transition—asserting, for example, that counselors "don't need to be shoving it in your face," "shoving [information] down our throats," or, in an Atlanta man's terms, "pushing you into it" and "brainwashing" students. "I felt forced … to go to college," a Latina concludes. "I have to do something that I'd really rather not do."

As a Baltimore high school student vividly describes it,

> I think America just needs to … put all of us kids on fingers and make us puppets and say "you're going to get straight As, you're going to go to college, you're going to lead a perfect life." … . And it's not true. You need to just back off a little bit and let us choose for ourselves. They're pushing us into things, and when we get into them and we decide we hate them, and then we decide we hate life … . You just need to let us make our own decisions.

Perhaps because they felt forced into a high school to college transition, some of the focus group participants felt that college was a direction without a goal. "I don't know exactly why I'm going to college," one recent high school graduate confesses. She adds, "I know that I want to get a job. But everyone says, 'go to college,' so I'm going to college." Says a college freshman, "I kind of feel like I'm working towards nothing. I'm working in college, but what is that going to?"

Looking Back

Retrospectively, some older women returning to school for advanced degrees echoed the same insights about their transition, years earlier, from high school to college. "I did what my family told me to do," one recalls. "You try to bring home good grades, and you're not really doing it for yourself. You're doing it to please everybody else. And I think that's one thing, as you get older, you learn: you've got to satisfy yourself." Some Work to College women who were on an early spiral toward college and were seeking postgraduate degrees admitted that they now admire kids who "had the courage to say, 'wait a minute, this isn't quite what I want.' … . I didn't have that much courage."

Gaining a Foothold

Many students feel that they are asked to make an irrevocable decision about college without a clear appreciation of their options and the consequences of their choices. Some students on the spiral toward college report feeling pressured or "shoved" into it, without a clear understanding of their own goals or of career alternatives. Hence, in focus groups many also reported an anesthetized, passive attitude toward their future, describing their feelings as "blank" or "listless." Students on the spiral away from college, in contrast, report that they had too little information and encouragement to secure their foothold in higher education. In either case, focus group research suggests that young women moving out of high school differ from older women returning to college in that they do not describe as much genuine, active decision making or efficacy about their educational transition, as the next chapter will elaborate.

Decision Making and "Forces Beyond My Control"

■

Significantly more women than men who moved from high school to full-time work feel that the decision not to attend college was based on circumstances or "forces beyond their control" (26% to 15%). Fewer women than men feel that the decision was "basically their own choice."

Not only do more women than men feel that a decision about college was thwarted by forces beyond their control, but that sentiment is also more prevalent among lower-income respondents and those caring for a child when they graduated from high school. Respondents who cited financial reasons for not continuing their education, of course, were significantly more likely to say that the decision was due to forces beyond their control.

Lack of Interest or Lack of Opportunity?

Male high school graduates who moved directly into full-time employment are more likely than their female counterparts to report that they were "never interested in college," and that this lack of interest was a "very important" factor in their decision. In other words, they are more likely to feel that their decision not to go directly to college reflected their own lack of interest, rather than mitigating circumstances or exigencies.

Only 15 percent of the women in the School to Work group report as a "very important" reason for not going to college that they were never interested in college, significantly lower than the 26 percent of the men who cite lack of interest as a very important

reason. Eighty-two percent (82%) of women in this group had seriously considered going to college, significantly higher than the 70 percent of men who had seriously considered it.

Correspondingly, significantly more men report as a "very important" deciding factor a belief that they "do not need college to get a decent job" after high school (24% of men, 14% of women). And, in fact, a much higher percentage of school to work men do consider their work to be a "career" (51% of men to 29% of women), while substantially more women report that their work is "just a job" (67% of women, 47% of men).

Finally, a significantly higher percentage of School to College men report that they "feel like [they] got pushed into college by other people" and "never really made the decision [themselves]" (17% of men, 8% of women).

Of the students who feel that the decision to go to work rather than college was based on matters beyond their control, a vast majority cite financial constraints, and almost four in 10 cite the responsibilities of caring for children or other relatives.

The Gender Gap in College Enrollment Revisited

Although more women than men are currently enrolled in higher education (55% versus 45%), many of these women are returning students rather

The School to Work Transition
(differences by sex)

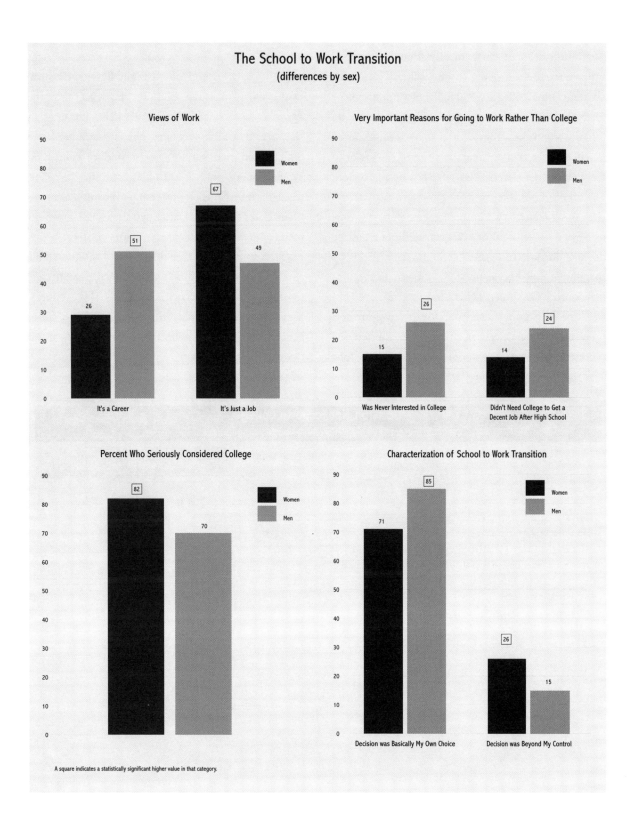

Views of Work

- It's a Career: Women 26, Men 51
- It's Just a Job: Women 67, Men 49

Very Important Reasons for Going to Work Rather Than College

- Was Never Interested in College: Women 15, Men 26
- Didn't Need College to Get a Decent Job After High School: Women 14, Men 24

Percent Who Seriously Considered College

- Women 82, Men 70

Characterization of School to Work Transition

- Decision was Basically My Own Choice: Women 71, Men 85
- Decision was Beyond My Control: Women 26, Men 15

Women
Men

A square indicates a statistically significant higher value in that category.

than students going immediately from high school into college.[6] Among high school students contemplating college, women are significantly more likely to say that not going to college is based on forces beyond their control, and are also significantly less likely than men to view their jobs as careers or to feel that college is unnecessary for getting a good job.

Are young men correct in their assessments that they can "get a decent job" or a "career" without a college degree? Research suggests that in some fields, a thriving "sub-baccalaureate" job market has developed. Computer fields, for example, reward skills rather than credentials and have created lucrative entry level positions for students—predominantly male—without college degrees. Jobs in mechanical trades, especially, continue to offer generous salaries and are also predominantly male fields. Other research cautions, however, that the demand for college-educated workers continues to rise, and that access to elite jobs is becoming more difficult for men without postsecondary education. Women in Atlanta, for example, according to recent research on the economy, enjoy incomes that are rising faster than men's, although they still lag behind men's incomes. "Too many southern men," this research summarizes, "see their careers based on their ability to do specific things: make things, drive things, dig things, lift things, or pick things. The economy, meanwhile, is rewarding those—regardless of race, gender, and ethnicity—who have the ability to think things."[7]

Decision Not to Go to College (percent saying decision not to go to college was)		
	Beyond Their Control	Their Own Choice
College is too expensive	89	59
A lack of money or financial aid	80	59
Caring for children or other relatives at the time	42	23
Never interested in college	34	57

A square indicates a statistically significant higher value in that category.

Goals,

Aspirations,

Rationales

THE DUAL AGENDA OF ECONOMIC SUCCESS AND SELF-FULFILLMENT

The survey research shows that women have a "dual agenda" for attending college. Whether going to college straight from high school or after working for some time, they attend college for both economic (career, income) and self-fulfillment (personal enrichment) reasons. Although economics and fulfillment are essential reasons for both women and men to continue their education, women place more emphasis on self-fulfillment than do men.

A majority of School to College women cite economic goals for college, including, "to help obtain a well paying or better paying job or career" and "to increase [my] income." Self-fulfillment reasons deemed "very important" by at least 49 percent of the School to College women include "for personal enrichment and satisfaction," "to become a more informed member of society," and "to interact with people from diverse backgrounds." School to College women are significantly more likely than men to deem these reasons very important.

Notably, as indicated in the table below, **there are several significant differences by sex in the School to College segment, yet fewer differences by sex—and none that are significant—in the Work to College segment's descriptions of their goals.** Men and women who have been in the workforce and are returning to school, that is, differ less in their goals than young men and women in high school.

Motivators for Attending College (percent who cite as a "very important" reason for attending college)	School to College		Work to College	
	Women	Men	Women	Men
Pursue a career that is interesting and personally fulfilling	91	86	90	85
For personal enrichment	80	(67)	85	78
WTC: Obtain a better-paying job, position, or career / STC: Obtain a well-paying job, position, or career	77	70	69	61
Increase income	n/a	n/a	56	54
Become a more informed member of society	62	(46)	52	50
Move to a completely different line of work	n/a	n/a	46	48
Interact with people from diverse backgrounds	49	(33)	33	25
Parents/family expected me to	41	(31)	13	5
Improve social status or image	16	13	9	14
Sibling influence	14	9	9	8

A circle indicates a statistically significant lower value within that category.

The item most often mentioned as the single most important motivator among both the School to College and Work to College groups is "to pursue a career that is interesting and fulfilling." This reason gets to the heart of the dual agenda, as it integrates the search for personal fulfillment into the pursuit of a career and, presumably, financial security and economic self-sufficiency. Women and men in both college-bound segments also chose "to obtain a well paying job, position, or career," "for personal enrichment and satisfaction," and "to give yourself more choices in life" as the other single most important reasons for pursuing postsecondary education.

In the qualitative research, women's goals of achieving economic self-sufficiency and securing "interesting and fulfilling" work typically appeared mutually reinforcing and intermeshed. "I started taking classes for my own personal enrichment to start with, with the second emphasis being that I could probably get a promotion out of this," an Altoona low-income woman explains. A Chicago returning student recognizes that she will "get credit which goes toward the pay scale" for her program, but "that's not why I took it. I took it because I got to speak French for two weeks [and] … meet other teachers."

Different Students, Similar Goals: Comparing Traditional and Nontraditional Students

Although the nontraditional* college student population continues to grow, there may be a misperception of why older students return to school. The idea that nontraditional students return to school to learn specific, targeted skills or to further their careers overlooks the desire for personal fulfillment and enrichment that women, especially, cite as strong motivators for returning to school.

In fact, the pragmatic view of a college diploma as a credential, a "piece of paper that one must have" to open doors in life, is much more prevalent among younger respondents—those in the School to College group and those who returned to college before age 25 in the Work to College group—than it is among the returning students generally and those over 25. This may be due to the larger percentage of younger students who are pursuing bachelor's degrees, often considered the "basic" post-high school degree requirement.

In addition, those in the Work to College group who are people of color, have average or below average high school grades, or are currently enrolled in a two-

Getting the Credential (percent who cite as a "very important" goal)	School to College		Work to College			
	Women	Men	Women	Men	Less than 25 years Old	More than 25 years Old
The need to get the diploma—the piece of paper—that is key to getting so many things out of life	59	60	38	38	45	31

A square indicates a statistically significant higher value in that category.

* "Nontraditional" students include those who are older than those students transitioning directly out of high school to college, and students who are pursuing degrees at a different pace than the four-year, full-time matriculation.

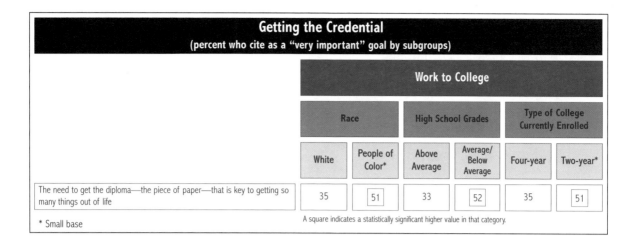

	Work to College					
Getting the Credential (percent who cite as a "very important" goal by subgroups)	**Race**		**High School Grades**		**Type of College Currently Enrolled**	
	White	People of Color*	Above Average	Average/ Below Average	Four-year	Two-year*
The need to get the diploma—the piece of paper—that is key to getting so many things out of life	35	51	33	52	35	51

* Small base

A square indicates a statistically significant higher value in that category.

year college are significantly more likely to say that the need for the "piece of paper" is a very important reason for going to college.

"Quality-of-Career" Issues

Work to College participants in the focus groups, as in the quantitative research, drew on more multifaceted and richer paradigms than their School to College counterparts to explain why they valued education and made the decision to return to school. One recurring perspective emphasized "quality-of-career" issues. These women saw education as a way to boost earning power, and also as a way to find a career that would have authentic, inherent value and satisfaction for them. "You always look for something that you do simply because you want to do it," a Chicago returning student muses, "and you don't care if you make five bucks or $50,000. That's what I felt." Low-income women in Altoona also strongly emphasized education as a means to achieve quality-of-careers goals. "I worked in a factory for eight years before I went back to school," recalls one, and "I just knew that there was something more that I wanted to do, something that I enjoyed doing, not something that I had to do." Says a Chicago woman, "I woke up dreading going into work. This is boring. I don't want to do this anymore ... I'm spending my life doing it,

and I need to do something else. And in order to find that, I had to go back to school."

A related Work to College perspective stresses postsecondary education as "a ticket out of being subservient" and a way to "go beyond ourselves," as an African American returning student describes. Work to College women sometimes emphasized education as a path to personal autonomy and economic independence, either from a husband or an employer. The desire for independence from the vicissitudes of downsizing and employers' whims was especially vivid in the group of low-income women, who underscore that "you don't want to have to depend on anybody but yourself." One wants to work "for herself" because she has "been let down by employers so much."

Finally, among higher-income women returning to school, one popular perspective views education almost as a "selfish" act or pleasure, a dream deferred that a woman pursues for her own fulfillment rather than for the needs of her children or career. "It's something that you're not doing for others, but that you're doing for yourself, to make you happy," a Chicago woman elaborates, "something that maybe at one time had been cut short for hundreds of reasons; for whatever the reasons may be, now you're not doing it to get promoted, you're not doing it to get

> **"** [I will go to college] for fun, inspiration. I want to be inspired by all my teachers, because up until this year, I really haven't been inspired. I love going to school right now, and it is the best feeling in the world, so I want to make sure that's what **"** it's like in college.
>
> —Los Angeles, Latina, high school senior

more money … . It's really something deeper than that." "I got married and basically did for my family and did for my kids. And actually it was really hard for me to kind of be selfish," another explains, "but I'm looking at things now that I want to do for me."

A Persistence of Goals

The findings in both the survey and focus groups caution that the view of younger students as interested primarily in learning for learning's sake and of older students as pragmatists in search of specific career-enhancing skills may not reflect the aspirations and goals that inspire women and men to return to school. Almost eight out of 10 women in both college-bound groups—and significantly more women than men in the School to College group—choose "personal enrichment" as a very important goal. The "dual agenda" is an especially strong motivator among female students, and it persists—in fact grows stronger—in the Work to College context.

Obstacles

and

Barriers

THE STORY OF MONEY

■

One of the most significant obstacles to a college education is a lack of money or financial aid. This is true for all three groups polled, but especially for the Work to College and School to Work segments. However, **although money matters to all students undergoing or contemplating an educational transition, it matters differently for men and women in some key respects.**

Lack of Money and Lack of Information about Money

According to the survey, **over one-half of the School to College group and about two-thirds in each of the other two groups say that "a lack of money or financial aid" is an obstacle to going to college.**

In the School to Work group, women are significantly more likely than men to say that a lack of financial resources is a barrier to education (69% of women, 55% of men), and that college is too expensive for them (71% of women, 58% of men). They are also significantly more likely than men to feel that "more financial aid for anyone who needs it" would have made them much more likely to attend (60% of women, 45% of men).

Students whose parents did not attend college are more likely to say money was a barrier to college. The spirals away from and toward college are evident, then, in the dual effects of parental education and income on children's financial access to college.

Although focus group respondents in some instances lamented their own lack of preparation or motivation to go to college, they were unanimous in their frustration that financial need alone curtails some people's educational options and aspirations. "We should just abolish money right now," advocates a Baltimore high school participant.

Several respondents asserted that an education is worth the money allocated to financial aid, and that "everyone [who] has aspirations" to get an education should be able to fulfill them. "I vote for giving all the money kids need to get smart," declares an Altoona participant.

Financial Obstacles: Effect of Parents' Education (percent who cite as an obstacle)	School to College		Work to College		School to Work	
	High School or Less	Some College +	High School or Less	Some College +	High School or Less	Some College +
A lack of money and/or financial aid	61	48	74	62	63	60

A square indicates a statistically significant higher value in that category.

Financial Obstacles: Effect of Household Income (percent who cite as an obstacle)						
	School to College		Work to College		School to Work	
	Household Income		Income When Attended College		Income When Graduated From High School	
	Under $50,000	$50,000 or more	Under $30,000	$30,000 or more	Under $40,000	$40,000 or more
A lack of money and/or financial aid	75	38	68	65	74	42

A square indicates a statistically significant higher value in that category.

Women are also significantly more likely than men to say that better, or more user-friendly, information about financial aid—more accessible processes for securing fellowships, loans, or aid, and more user-friendly bureaucratic structures—would have made them "much more likely" to go to college (51% of women, 33% of men). Indeed, other research shows that returning students, in particular, must familiarize themselves with and assess a bewildering array of federal, state, and local aid options, and many different kinds of aid, including grants, loans, federal work-study programs, professional scholarships, and so on.[8]

Credit Card Debt

According to the Institute for Higher Education Policy, the typical recent college graduate who borrowed to pay for college has monthly debt

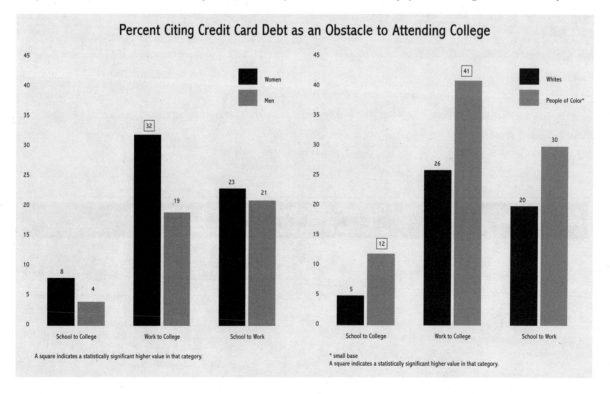

Percent Citing Credit Card Debt as an Obstacle to Attending College

A square indicates a statistically significant higher value in that category.

* small base
A square indicates a statistically significant higher value in that category.

payment totaling $852, including an average of $678 in noneducational debt. Sixty-seven percent (67%) of college students had credit cards in 1996. Reflecting trends toward larger debt burdens at earlier ages, a surprising number of survey respondents say that credit card debt was an obstacle to continuing their education.[9]

Women in the Work to College group are significantly more likely than men to say that credit card debt was a barrier to going to college. The incidence of credit card debt as an obstacle is highest in the School to Work and the Work to College groups, where approximately one-quarter to one-third of women, respectively, cite it as a factor in their decision.

Focus group participants echoed the survey results. Women recalled having been targeted for new credit cards upon high school graduation, and quickly having become overextended. "I learned about something called 'bills,'" reminisces a Baltimore student recently out of high school. "When you are in college, telemarketers call you and send you a credit card, and you are stupid enough to get it. And you are in debt thousands of dollars … . I have bills and other bills like credit cards." An Atlanta woman moving from Work to College confesses that she and her husband use credit cards to "live beyond [their] means. I could have gotten a credit card with a real low limit," she recalls, "but I liked the shiny gold one … . Walk into Rich's and buy something and hand them a plain credit card, or hand them the shiny gold card. Which are you going to get better service out of?"

In the Work to College focus groups, especially, some women said that returning to school was contingent on paying off the loans and debts they had already accumulated, often on credit cards. "I saved for two years, paid off my car, paid off credit cards, and saved

> "
> *Money talks. It really does. When I was 21 I got these cards. I'm 26 now and I've got $5,000 on one card that* "
> *I'm having to pay off.*
>
> —Atlanta, African American, Work to School

money to go back," reports an Altoona, Pennsylvania, Work to College student.

Anxiety about Debt

Other research has found that women tend to make more conservative financial decisions than men. It is possible that women have more anxiety about credit card and student loan debt, even if they do not have greater debt than men, or that they are more "debt-averse" than men when it comes to student loans. The UCLA Freshman Survey of 1999 did find that significantly more women—nearly 71%—were at least somewhat concerned about financing their college education, compared to 58% of men.

Alternately, women may assign more importance to debt in their deliberations about educational transitions. In the focus groups, several participants contemplating a college transition, either directly out of high school or after having worked, worried about projected debt. "It is going to be really expensive," a Los Angeles Latina predicts, "and that is what worries me about the future. How am I going to pay for all of that?" Others feared the lingering burden of debt. "With the interest even larger," an African American woman laments, "I'll be paying this off for years."

ANXIETIES: THE STORY OF SELF-FULFILLING PROPHECIES

∎

At least four types of anxiety about the college experience appear to impede college attendance:

- The academic requirements of college
- SAT scores
- Social issues at college
- High school grades

Anxiety About Academic Preparation

The source of anxiety most often cited as an obstacle to attending college is "nervousness about the academic requirements," mentioned by about half of the women in the School to College and Work to College groups and four in 10 women in the School to Work group.

Male students, students who are people of color, and students from families with a household income under $40,000 are all significantly more **likely to be deterred from college by anxiety about the admissions and selection process.** Twenty percent of School to Work men, for example, in comparison with nine percent of School to Work women, named "thought it was too difficult to get accepted into college" as a "very important" obstacle.

Concern about high school grades is highest among respondents who did not go to college, that is, the School to Work group. People of color in this group were more likely to feel that their grades were too low for them to apply to college.

In focus group conversations, Latina and African American women leaving high school were concerned that the college admissions and selection process would be too "competitive" and that this process would initiate future competitive challenges. "I feel like I have to do better than everybody else, so I have to work harder," explains an African American

Sources of Anxiety by Sex (percent who cite as an obstacle)						
	School to College		Work to College		School to Work	
	Women	Men	Women	Men	Women	Men
Academic requirements at college	54	45	46	44	40	32
SAT scores	34	22	25	25	30	38
Social life at college	36	26	14	24	21	20
High school grades	16	16	17	25	36	47

A square indicates a statistically significant higher value in that category.

student in Los Angeles. Latina participants, in particular, vividly imagined the cutthroat, competitive nature of college admissions. "After college," a Latina School to Work student argues, "you still have to compete in college ranks, so … unless you are valedictorian at Harvard, you are always going to have some type of competition."

Another Latina student recently out of high school expressed anxiety about feeling academically inferior to her classmates. "How many years have I been in school?" she questions, "I feel stupid. I feel like I haven't learned anything at all … I have, but I feel stupid and I see all these smart people … I know a lot of people [in] their freshman year of college, they drop out. That is one of my fears … once I get past that first year, I'm set."

Placing Anxiety in Context

Anxieties about academic preparation, performance, and grades may become self-fulfilling prophecies. Not only do they deter attendance at college in the first place, as this survey research shows, but they may also affect academic achievement for those who do persist. Recent research has shown that "stereotype anxiety," or beliefs about who succeeds or fails in school, can influence a student's performance. For example, a female student's expectation that she will do poorly in math may affect her grade on a test, and vice versa. It is possible that anxiety about low performance leads students to overestimate the competitiveness or difficulty of college, thus deterring them from applying in the first place.[10]

> " *You have to get a job, to get into college, to get the skills, to get the job that makes good money, to get the mansion.* "
>
> —Baltimore suburb, African American, high school senior

College Admissions Tests

∎

Context

The dismantling of affirmative action policies by some state university systems has reinvigorated a perennial debate about the weight and validity of standardized tests such as the PSAT, SAT, and ACT in the college admissions process. Critics of the tests cite potential bias against people of color and women in the test design—as manifested in significant gaps in scores between the sexes and races—and the SAT's uneven value as a predictor of college grades.[11] Advisors to the University of California system, among others, have recommended making SAT scores an optional part of the college application, or phasing them out of admissions considerations entirely, to compensate for potential post-affirmative action decreases in Hispanic and African American enrollment. Raymund Paredes, vice-chancellor of UCLA, explains, "there is a growing sense of concern around the country that without affirmative action to mitigate the effects of the SATs, we're forced to look at the consequences of the SATs more directly."[12]

Findings

This survey research shows that many prospective students—especially women and people of color—certainly perceive the admissions tests to be of dubious validity, and name them as an obstacle to college. Approximately one-quarter to one-third of women in each of the three transition groups say that anxiety about SAT scores is an obstacle to college.

In the School to College group, women are significantly more likely than men to cite SAT scores as an obstacle.

School to Work high school graduates who are people of color also point to the SATs as an obstacle to pursuing college: 37 percent of the School to Work graduates of color, as compared to 20 percent of the white graduates, feel that "getting rid of standardized tests such as the SATs" would have made them "much more likely" to go to college.

Unfair and Inaccurate?

In addition to serving as a source of anxiety and an obstacle for some women, standardized college admissions tests such as the SAT or ACT are seen as unfair and biased by a majority of the women, even those who went on to college directly out of high school. **Women in the School to College and Work to College groups are significantly more likely than men to criticize the fairness and accuracy of the tests and their ability to predict how a student will do in college.**

Over half of the women in the Work to College group and almost half in the other two groups think that people who can afford preparation classes have an unfair advantage. Only about one-third of either women or men in any of the groups agree that the tests accurately predict how students will do in college.

In a focus group of 14 African American high school students, all but two expressed concern about SAT scores as a barrier to college. One participant in the group explains that she joined the Marines because "I didn't really want to have to deal with having all these schools to compete with, and all these people to compete with and taking the SATs a million times, and trying to get a perfect score." Another echoes, "I was worried about whether my SAT scores would be high enough, what college I would attend, and if I got the right grades."

Significantly, these students were impeded from applying to college by anxieties about the possibility of low scores, not by low scores themselves.

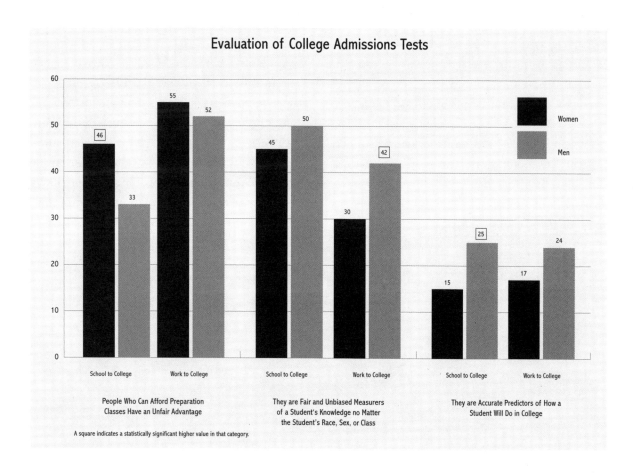

Evaluation of College Admissions Tests

People Who Can Afford Preparation Classes Have an Unfair Advantage

They are Fair and Unbiased Measurers of a Student's Knowledge no Matter the Student's Race, Sex, or Class

They are Accurate Predictors of How a Student Will Do in College

A square indicates a statistically significant higher value in that category.

Social Anxieties and the Treatment of Women and Minorities in Higher Education

■

On the whole, women in all three transition groups perceive college as an inviting place. Few cite "society's attitude toward women" or the "treatment of women in higher education" as explicit obstacles. **But college appears somewhat less inviting for people of color, one-third of whom feel that college is tougher for them than it is for white students.**

About one-fifth of women in the two college-bound groups agree that "society's attitude toward women and education" or the "treatment of women in the higher education system" were obstacles to continuing their education.

About one-third of the people of color in the School to College and Work to College groups agree that the "treatment of racial and ethnic minorities in the higher education system" was an obstacle to continuing their education.

Women who did go from high school to college also did not feel that college was a "tougher place for women than it is for men." School to Work women's and men's opinions are similar on this point (18% of women agree, 16% of men agree). A higher percentage—about one-quarter of women in the School to Work group—agree that "college is a tougher place for ethnic and racial minorities than it is for whites."

Social Life in College

Nervousness about social life at college is more of a concern to students in the School to College group than to respondents in the other two groups. **Men are significantly more likely than women in the Work to College group to say nervousness about social life is an obstacle to going to college. Men in the School to Work group are significantly more likely to say that it was a very important factor in their decision not to go to college** (8% of men, 3% of women).

GUIDANCE Counselors: A Missed Opportunity?

■

Guidance counselors receive mixed reviews from all three transition groups surveyed. Students with below-average grades report receiving less time and attention than they needed from counselors.

Guidance counselors are a potentially powerful force that might intervene to minimize some of the differences between students whose parents attended college and those whose parents did not. Thirty-seven percent of the School to College group whose parents had a high school education or less say their guidance counselor was a very influential source of information, versus 24% of those whose parents had at least a college education. Those whose parents went to college relied more on their parents than on guidance counselors.

Overworked and Understaffed

The mixed reviews may stem from the fact that guidance counselors are overworked and understaffed, especially in public schools. Research by The College Board in 1986 forewarned of a counselor crisis, when it found that some counselors have to deal with a caseload of as many as 700 students and

that many are assigned an array of administrative and record keeping tasks that severely curtail their actual counseling time—a trend confirmed by the American School Counselor Association. Students who need information the most, the research concluded, are the least likely to get it, as they often attend crowded, urban schools with the highest student-to-counselor ratios. Thus, the spirals are reinforced, as students whose parents attended college receive more information in school, and others receive less. Research in 1999 confirms that the understaffing of counselors constitutes a missed opportunity to equip

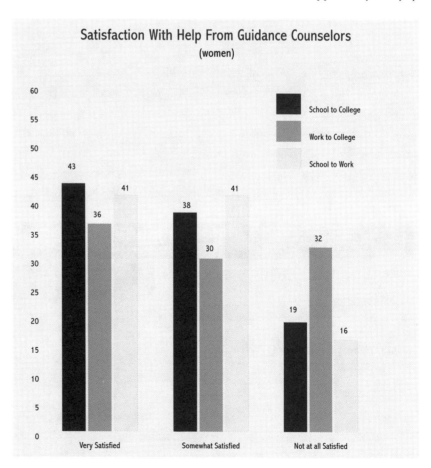

Satisfaction With Help From Guidance Counselors
(women)

School to College
Work to College
School to Work

	Very Satisfied	Somewhat Satisfied	Not at all Satisfied
School to College	43	38	19
Work to College	36	30	32
School to Work	41	41	16

the nontraditional or first-generation student to make an informed decision about college. McDonough (1999) finds that counselors do indeed have a strong impact on the colleges to which students apply and the institutions they eventually attend, in schools where the student-to-counselor ratio is low and/or college counseling is given more attention.[13]

Major Complaints Regarding Guidance Counselors

There are few variations by race in how students describe their experiences with counselors. However, significantly more students who self-report that they had "below average grades" feel that guidance counselors did not give them enough time or attention. This response is especially prevalent among men with below average grades, who may not conform to a counselor's image of "college material."

Women who went directly to college are most likely to have met with a high school guidance counselor, while those who did not go to college are the least likely. Women in each of the groups report somewhat mixed levels of satisfaction with the help they received from their guidance counselors. And even among students who proceed directly from high school to college, 41 percent are only "somewhat satisfied" with their counseling experience, while 18 percent are "not satisfied at all."

Approximately one-fifth to one-third of the women in each of the groups think their counselor could have spent more time with them and could have been better informed. This assessment is particularly apparent among students with average or below-average high school grades.

Academic Triage

Several respondents in the focus groups had especially vivid feelings about their interactions with guidance counselors. "You go in and you talk to your guidance counselor," one recalls, "and … you tell them what you want to be when you grow up or whatever. I told her I want to be a marine biologist and she said no, … you can't do that … you don't have the grades for it … you'll never make it. But I stuck it out by ignoring her and I'm a marine biology and psychology major." Some respondents described a process of academic triage, necessitated perhaps by the limited resources of time, staff, and money confronting many public school counselors. A Washington, D.C., public school student—who was

The Guidance Counselor Experience (percent who agree)			
	School to College	Work to College*	School to Work
Guidance counselor didn't give them the time or attention needed	21	32	23
Guidance counselor wasn't well informed	27	33	15
Guidance counselors do a good job informing students about college	68	47	67

A square indicates a statistically significant higher value in that category.
A circle indicates a statistically significant lower value in that category.

Note: The base is women who met with their guidance counselor and graduated from high school in the last five years.

accepted at an Ivy League university despite her counselor's initial lack of attention—speculates on her counselor's philosophy: "It's like a survival of the fittest type thing. If she doesn't think highly of you, then she selects you out of [college information]."[14]

A major complaint in focus groups was not so much that counselors lacked the time for students and did not give them any input, but that counselors told them only what they could not do, rather then telling them how they could achieve an educational goal eventually, even if not immediately after high school.

A Baltimore high school graduate remembers asking her principal about college: "It wasn't that he was knocking me down," she says, "but he said, 'your grades don't really prove too much.' And I was like, where do you go with that? He [said] 'your SAT scores and your grades aren't high enough. You can just go to community college,' and then he just told me to leave. It wasn't in a mean way, but he was just like, he had some other stuff to do. Like I had no choice but to go to a community college." A Latina recounts a similar experience with her guidance counselor: "You go in and you tell her what you want to do, and she'll tell you you can't do it. She picked over all our stuff and said, 'no, you can't do that.' I told her I wanted to do something in medicine, and she's like, 'nope, you can't. I'm sorry.'" Another high school student reports that the counselor "pushes" college on students. "He's not asking you if you're going to college. He says, 'I'm going to go over what colleges you can probably get in to.' "

"What Kind of 'Material' We Are"

Several women and some men in the focus groups felt that they were told what sort of "material" they were as people, rather than being given information and guidance about their immediate educational and

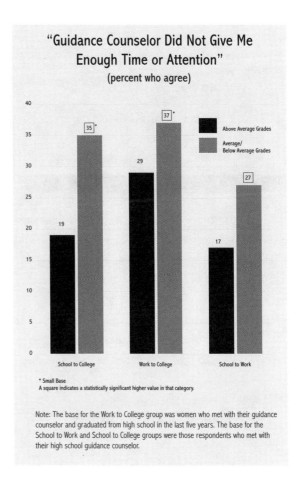

"Guidance Counselor Did Not Give Me Enough Time or Attention"
(percent who agree)

* Small Base
A square indicates a statistically significant higher value in that category.

Note: The base for the Work to College group was women who met with their guidance counselor and graduated from high school in the last five years. The base for the School to Work and School to College groups were those respondents who met with their high school guidance counselor.

occupational decisions and choices. As a Baltimore high school student tells it, "My mom went in for a meeting with the teachers, and they were like, 'your daughter is community college material.' Well, she took that as an insult … . She thought they were basically putting me down … . Why are they saying what kind of 'material' we are?" Students are also aware that they may be performing below their potential, and are dubious when counselors see their grades as reflections of their inherent academic abilities. An Atlanta Work to College student remembers that her counselor advised her to take remedial classes "because I made a lower grade on my English class. But I made a lower grade because I never went! That was her first thought, that I should take [remedial courses]."

> "
> *The college counselor tells you what you can't do, which is [sometimes what you] want to do.*
> "
>
> —Los Angeles, Latina, high school senior

A few focus group participants explained how they persevered despite their counselor's bleak assessments. A Latina participant concedes that she had low grades in high school, but found that her counselor was "not supportive at all. I still thought I could do whatever I really wanted to, and she just didn't advise me to apply to any of my colleges. Even though I did, and I got accepted to every single one."

Contexts and Conclusions

The projected "knowledge economy" of the 21st century will reward those who are equipped to learn as capable "students" throughout their lives, in both formal and informal learning environments. In many respects, however, the transition to college is described as a discrete, one-shot experience for students graduating from high school, a transition for which they are either qualified or not. The possibility of students combining work with a few college classes after high school, or of preparing themselves to spiral back in to college after a few years of work does not appear to be an option that schools present or emphasize. Instead, students reported having been told whether or not they were "college material" in a general sense, and then steered immediately toward college or away from it. Without sufficient staff or time, it is undoubtedly difficult for guidance counselors to help students thoughtfully map out long-term career and education objectives or plans. This research suggests that high school graduates who self-report that they received "below average" grades or who do not have family encouragement to go to college are receiving a message that postsecondary education is not a realistic goal. Yet it will be important for students, counselors, and teachers to take a longer view of educational transitions and options: Even if an initial transition from high school to college seems unlikely due to grades, academic preparation, lack of interest, or financial problems, students leaving high school should be equipped and feel competent to "spiral in" to postsecondary education and learning in the long term.

THE Information Gap

■

There is a strong need for more information about the entire college application and selection process, particularly for students whose parents did not go to college, those with low incomes or from lower-income families, and those who enrolled in two-year colleges. Of the School to Work group, **72 percent feel that better information about colleges, degrees, and programs would have made them somewhat or much more likely to attend, and 60 percent of the Work to College segment favor more information about colleges, degrees, and programs, in order to make education more accessible.**

Parents are a critical source of information about college, even for students returning to school from the workforce, and parents with a college degree are more likely to supply this information, thus reinforcing the spiral toward college.

What They Don't Know May Hurt Them: Information and the Quality of Decisions

Substantial percentages of respondents in each of the three groups believe that high schools need to improve the amount and quality of information available to students so that they may make better choices about colleges and careers. Almost one in two School to Work respondents agree that they could have made a better decision if they had more information, in comparison with about 40 percent of the two college-bound groups.

In all three transition groups, **women are significantly more likely than men to agree that better sources of information would have influenced their decision.** For example, one in three School to Work men report that "better sources of information" would have had "no effect at all" on their decision not to go to college, but only one in five School to Work women feel this way.

		School to College Group				
	Family Income		**High School Grades**		**SAT Scores**	
	Under $50,000	$50,000 or more	Above Average	Average/Below Average	Above Average	Average/Below Average
Percent who say that they could have made better decisions about college if they had had better information	47	33	33	59	33	46
Percent who say that much more information needs to be made available to high school students to help them make better decisions about college and careers	94	80	80	95	79	92

Need for Information
(by income, grades, SAT scores)

A square indicates a statistically significant higher value in that category.

Students with "below-average" grades and SAT scores and who come from families with incomes under $50,000 are significantly more likely to feel that better information could have improved their decisions about college. Income, grades, and SAT scores have a similar impact on the Work to College group, although the differences are not significant in this group.

Money, Knowledge, and Power

School to College

Even among students who went from high school directly to college, most feel that they did not know very much about the college selection and application process. This is particularly true of men.

Two sociodemographic factors have a strong influence on the knowledge level of the School to College group: income and the parents' level of education. Consistent with the spiral toward college, nearly half of respondents whose family income is $50,000 or more say they knew a lot about the college selection and application process, with only one-quarter of respondents who come from families with less than $50,000 in annual income. Following the same pattern, close to half of respondents whose parents attended college say that they knew a lot, compared with less than one-third of those whose parents never attended college.

In terms of access to information outside of the family context, nothing succeeds like success: The spiral toward college includes better access to information

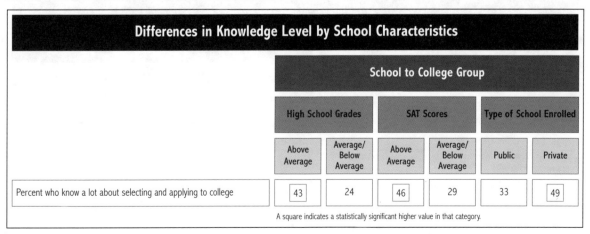

Differences in Knowledge Level by Family Characteristics

| | School to College Group | | | |
| | Household Income | | Parents' Education | |
	Less than $50,000	$50,000 or more	High School or Less	College
Percent who knew a lot about selecting and applying to college	25	46	30	43

A square indicates a statistically significant higher value in that category.

Differences in Knowledge Level by School Characteristics

| | School to College Group | | | | | |
| | High School Grades | | SAT Scores | | Type of School Enrolled | |
	Above Average	Average/ Below Average	Above Average	Average/ Below Average	Public	Private
Percent who know a lot about selecting and applying to college	43	24	46	29	33	49

A square indicates a statistically significant higher value in that category.

through higher grades and SAT scores, as shown on the preceding table.

Focus group participants recalled a deluge of mailings from colleges and universities trying to recruit them after they took their SATs or ACTs—provided they scored well enough. "You start getting flooded, just flooded, with information," a Chicago Work to College woman reports. The same situation applies to high grades, which some participants intuitively understood had granted them access to information. "As far as access to information [goes], I was a good student," another Chicago resident explains, "so I can't say that I felt like anything was held back."

Students who report knowing a lot about college are more likely to attend a four-year school, while those who do not know a lot are more likely to attend a two-year school.

Other research confirms high school students' intuition that they might have known more about the transition process. Olson's recent review of School to Work initiatives concludes emphatically that "most high school students have a fairly rosy view of their future careers that does not match the reality. Many receive little career counseling and have little sense of direction."[15]

Work to College

Just over half of the Work to College group say they knew a lot about the college selection and application process. While sex had no influence on the level of knowledge in this group, age did have an impact, with students aged 25 or older significantly more likely to know a lot about the process. Returning students who are older and have experience in the workforce have better access to information and/or

more skills with which to research the necessary information.

As with the School to College group, students in the Work to College group who had lower grades and/or SAT scores were generally less well informed about how to select and apply to colleges.

School to Work*

The overall level of knowledge about selecting and applying to college is much lower in the School to Work group than in the two college-bound groups. There are no significant differences among sociodemographic subgroups, except for educational attainment of parents.

Respondents in the School to Work group whose parents never attended college are much more likely to say they knew very little about selecting and applying to colleges. Those with a low level of knowledge are also much less likely to have met with a guidance counselor.

It is noteworthy that several participants in the focus groups saw access to information as perhaps the most precious advantage—even above money—held by children of college-educated, higher-income parents. As a participant in Atlanta explains, "There's something with parents. Either your parents have it or

> "
> *I don't know where to go.*
>
> *I don't know anything about college …*
> "
> *I don't know who to talk to.*
>
> —Baltimore, African American, high school senior

* Questions in this section were asked of School to Work respondents who had considered attending college.

they don't, and you can't control that … Information is out there for everybody now. I guess if you're coming from an information-driven family, then you know you have a lot of influential people in your life who will give you information that helps you from having to go out there and capture it yourself. That's a big advantage."

"Digging" for Information

For the most part, focus group participants conceded that the information is "out there," but believed that prospective students must "dig" for it themselves. Information, in other words, is perceived to be buried or hidden for those without ready access to it through their families. "They could have something that says when grants or scholarships [are available] … . You can get grants. But you have to really dig," comments a Latina high school student. A Chicago woman echoes, "I mean, theoretically, everyone got information, but you knew that wasn't it, and you knew who got more information about colleges and what kinds of grants were out there." Those who got information, she elaborates, were "the ones who always make it." While the high school may offer formal avenues of information, an African American Chicagoan clarifies, the real information is transmitted generationally: "The women in my family, all of them have degrees. They're very educated, so I knew choices, but it wasn't because high school gave me this information."

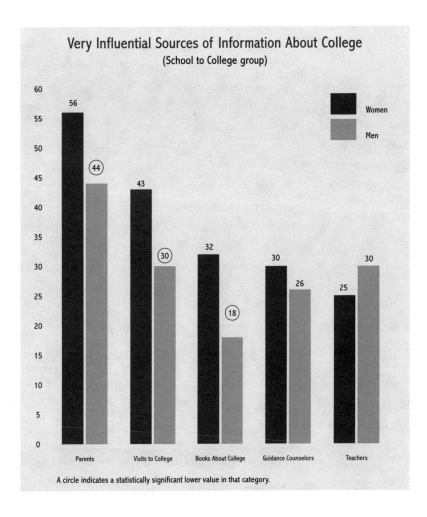

Very Influential Sources of Information About College
(School to College group)

A circle indicates a statistically significant lower value in that category.

The School to Work group has the highest percentage of women who had difficulty finding information about colleges, followed by the Work to College group. The School to College group had the least difficulty finding information.

Except for the School to Work group, differences between men and women are not significant. In the School to Work group, women are significantly more likely than men (43% to 26%) to say that they had a "difficult time getting adequate information" about selecting or applying to colleges.

Information About Careers

If information about college is hard to find, information about careers and career paths is no easier and, according to respondents in some groups, can be even harder to find. Twenty percent (20%) of students moving from high school to college agree that it was difficult to get information about college, but 32 percent agree that it was difficult to get information about careers. Equal percentages of the School to Work group—32 percent—agree that it was difficult to get information about both colleges and career options.

It is possible that the feeling of being "forced" or "pushed" that students on the spiral toward college described in focus group conversations was exacerbated by the (perhaps outdated) perception that the "vocational" option and the high school to career path are for remedial students who are not "college material." Yet several school systems in the late 1990s have recognized that some students may want to attend a technical school, community college, or pursue a high-paying, technical job rather than transition immediately from high school to a four-year college. These schools have integrated career and college prepa-

ration "tracks," such that "programs that involve job skills and a general career focus are becoming as integral a part of preparing for college [for many students] as taking math or science." Technology magnet schools in a Baltimore suburb, for example, focus on computer design, gene splicing, electric car design, and architecture, and provide a foundation for both college and career paths out of high school. The goal is not only to equip students for promising jobs after graduation, but also to help prospective college students clarify their own goals and possible career paths.[16]

Sources of Information About College (percent who said specific source was very influential)			
	School to College	Work to College	School to Work*
Parents	56	31	34
Visits to colleges	43	28	17
Books about college	32	24	19
Guidance counselors	30	7	27
Teachers	25	8	28
College representatives	20	13	16
Friends	17	16	19
Brother or sister	15	11	17
Other relative	14	7	–
The Internet	13	16	10
US News ratings	6	10	1
Spouse	1	10	6
Co-workers	n/a	8	8
Boss	n/a	4	9

A square indicates a statistically significant higher value in that category. A circle indicates a statistically significant lower value in that category.

*Asked of those who considered going to college

Influential Sources of Information

For women in the School to College group, parents are clearly the most influential source of information about college, followed by visits to colleges, books, guidance counselors, and teachers. Surprisingly, women rated books about college as "very influential" sources of information, more highly than teachers or guidance counselors.

> " *If you want [information], you can find it and research for it. But it is not like information is right there for you.* "
>
> —Altoona, PA, white, Work to School

Women are more eclectic in their decision making than men, as they are significantly more likely than men in the School to College group to say that parents, visits to colleges, and books about college were all "very influential" sources of information. However, students from upper-income households, predictably, rely more heavily on visits to college than do their lower-income counterparts.

Women think that other sources of information, such as college representatives, friends, the Internet, and *U.S. News and World Report* magazine ratings of colleges, are not particularly influential sources of information. However, it is important to realize that not all respondents had access to the Internet, so the percentage who say it is very influential may be understated.

Women in the School to Work group are less likely to rely on books about college as a source of information than are women in the School to College group.

Interactions

THE IMPACT OF LIFE TRANSITIONS ON EDUCATION

Age

Age is a stronger obstacle to returning to school for women than for men. Although adult students now account for nearly half of college enrollments overall, and students over 40 are the fastest-growing segment of the postsecondary population, some older women agreed in focus groups that they do not conform to the "traditional" view of the college student and that institutions have not adapted to meet demographic shifts in enrollment.[17]

About one-third of women in the Work to College group say that they are older than their fellow students, about one-fifth are married, and 15 percent were pregnant or responsible for the care of a child. Almost one in 10 women in the Work to College group is either recently divorced or caring for a relative.

Of the one-third of respondents in the Work to College group who say they are older than most other students in their classes, almost one in five of these women says that her age discouraged her from going to college (even though she eventually did). **It is interesting that age had much less influence on men, with fewer than 1 in 33 citing it as an obstacle (18% of women to 3% of men).**

Focus group participants observed the demographic trend toward older students ("There is a major trend in older students now. There [are] tons of older students in our classes, in all kinds of majors," a Work to College student observes), and some felt that they should receive more institutional support and

attention. "Unless they start structuring classes for adults instead of 18- to-22-year-olds," a Chicago Work to College participant asserts, "I really have no interest in it anymore ... because they approach kids completely differently than they would approach me ... and I just find it a little demeaning. The first day of this class, the professor's talking about going out, and getting drunk, and your parents ... and I'm thinking, 'what am I doing? I *am* the parent.' ... I just find the whole thing a bit off."

Work to College students in the survey report that college recruitment materials and information dissemination strategies that appeal to younger students do not appeal to or reach the growing

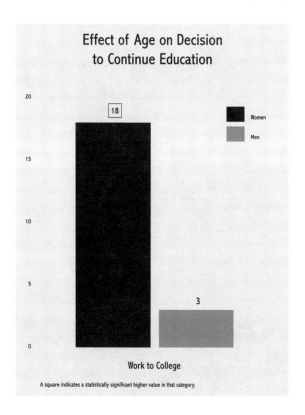

Effect of Age on Decision to Continue Education

20
18
15
10
5
0
Women
Men
3
Work to College

A square indicates a statistically significant higher value in that category.

population of older, returning students. The over-25 Work to College group is significantly less likely to feel that visits to campuses, visits from representatives, or books and printed materials on college would be even somewhat helpful in their decision making.

Marriage/Divorce and Family

Contingency Planning: "What if I Get Married and Have Kids?"

In focus groups, women described what researcher Karen Arnold calls "contingency planning"—a tendency for women to make decisions on the assumption that in the future they will have a family, be the primary caregivers, and will need to juggle many responsibilities and roles. This "virtual family" may shape some women's decisions even before they

> "
> *My parents didn't make a lot of money so obviously the fact that they had a good family is what kept them happy. I want to be able to do the same thing ... concentrate more on my family so that my family is happy regardless of what my job is. That is what made me put my goal together.*
> "
>
> —Altoona, PA, white, Work to School

find a partner or have children in reality. A white woman in Atlanta returning to school illustrates contingency planning around education and career: "If I lean toward ... becoming a teacher, you have summers off. And I figure that if I get married one day and I have children ... I'll want to take that time to invest with my children."[18]

Women in their 30s and 40s, however, remembering earlier transitions, had mixed feelings about linking their educational decisions to family, whether real or projected. A Chicago woman who returned to school laments that she "would have had more options" if she had pursued a career as an educator after high school. "I didn't realize that once I started a family, there were no options there ... I didn't have flexibility. I could have substituted. I could have had summers off, with my kids. So I wish I had been a little more focused and been able to see long term instead of just short term. My goals were very short term." An Altoona low-income woman tells a different story of switching to a business curriculum when she discovered she was pregnant: "I figured it would be easier, and I went to two years of college for business management. I was right ... . It was too easy. It was real boring for me." She returned to school because she felt that she had sacrificed too much to the exigencies of family at the expense of her inherent interest in her career.

Significantly, women typically explained how they would try to align their lives and career choices to the existing structures of higher education and family norms, rather than envisioning how educational and family structures might be made more compatible with their needs and schedules.

Reverse Contingency Planning: "What if I Get Divorced and Have Kids?"

Women in their 20s and 30s were just as likely to describe a kind of reverse contingency planning—mapping out educational and career options based on the possibility that they may get married, have a family, and then get divorced. Indeed, apprehension about divorce may inspire women to equip themselves through education to be economically self-sufficient, according to some focus group participants. "Many women depend on men," an Atlanta woman explains, "and if the man should ever leave you … you need some education … . And then, if he should ever leave, okay." As a Los Angeles woman elaborates, "I just want to be financially stable, just in case I get divorced. I just want to have a separate bank account … . I want to have everything straight."

Some of the research on the Work to School population confirms that a woman's educational transition may be inspired more by interpersonal displacement—principally divorce—than directly by economic or occupational displacement. Recent research on divorce, reentry women, and unemployment investigates whether economic uncertainty leads to greater enrollments in higher education, and whether there is a correlation between divorce rates and enrollment. Divorce rates show a positive relationship both to graduate and undergraduate enrollments of women in the United States but not in the United Kingdom. In both countries, the unemployment rate exerted a greater effect on the enrollment of men than on women. This study found that women's reentry was more responsive to changes in marital status than labor market changes in unemployment rates.[19]

Spouses as Sources of Support

Twenty-one percent (21%) of the married Work to School survey respondents report that "lack of spouse support" is a "significant obstacle" to continuing their education. However, when asked in an open-ended question to describe how being married affected their educational decision, the highest percentage of married respondents—32 percent—said that it had "no effect" on their transition.

> "
> *I think that if you were divorced or if you recently got divorced that would kind of give you motivation to go out and learn more and do something different.*
> "
>
> —Los Angeles, woman of color,
> Work to School, two-year college

In focus group research, although a few married women felt that their husbands provided emotional and financial support for them to make an educational transition, most did not mention husbands as particular sources of influence. Spouses appeared almost invisible in the discussion of how education and family interact, and women assumed that they would shoulder more responsibility than their husbands. "I know I'm going to have to go to work and come home and have more responsibilities as far as taking care of the kids, dinner, and all that," an Altoona woman explains, adding that "even if you do have a husband who participates … it is still not going to be as much as you do. The percentages are so spread apart. It is just insane."

The Paradox of Children

Children are a paradox in educational transitions: They provide a powerful incentive for women to seek postsecondary education, yet many institutions pose serious logistical and practical obstacles for women with children hoping to fulfill this educational goal.

> " *You know that if you have children, you need to be a good role model. You don't want to just have children. You want to show them that they can become something more. Instead of just being a housewife, I wanted to finish school to show them that is the way you need to do these things. You can't just be a housewife anymore.* "
>
> —Altoona, PA, white,
> Work to School, two-year college

Parents differ from their counterparts without children in some key respects. Respondents who are pregnant or caring for a child when they graduate from high school are more likely to wait until they are 25 or older before attending college, to enroll in a two-year college and to work as many or more hours than before they enrolled in college.

Parents Face Institutional Obstacles

Seventy-five percent of the School to Work group (men and women) who were pregnant or caring for children at the time they graduated from high school report that "having to care for children"

was a very important reason they did not go to college, and a vast majority—82 percent—name it as the "single most important" reason for not seeking a postsecondary education.

When asked to rate the importance of possible improvements in the delivery of higher education, 74 percent of the School to Work respondents with children say that day care would make them much more likely to attend, and one in five cites day care as the single most important factor that would encourage them to return to school. Returning students concur, with 74 percent of the Work to College group with children citing "more day care and schedules to accommodate students with children" as a "large help" in thinking about college, and fully 87 percent see it as at least somewhat of a help.

Time over Money?

Parents in the School to Work group may value day care services, time and flexibility—in the scheduling of classes and in length to degree completion requirements, for example—even above money as the most important changes that would have made them likely to go to college. When asked to identify the "single most important" thing that would have made them likely to go to college after high school, most of the School to Work group overall (28%) choose "more financial aid for anyone who needs it." However, among the subgroup with children, the highest percentage—26 percent—choose "more flexible scheduling of classes to accommodate outside demands," and the second-highest percentage choose "colleges offering day care services," at 19 percent. Another 19 percent name "more financial aid."

Other research corroborates the importance of flexible scheduling, particularly for Work to College women with children. In one study, returning women who did not persist cited conflicts in class scheduling and conflicts between work and school, as well as financial hardships. Another study, which recommended the establishment of informal support and assistance networks for returning parents, found that basic child care was less of a problem than exceptional needs for child care, such as in the case of a sick child, and an overall lack of time.[20]

In addition to reporting substantially more often that the decision to work was dictated by "forces beyond their control," **School to Work parents are significantly more likely to report that they received little to no encouragement from friends and spouses, and are more likely to report that parents and teachers were "not an influence at all" in giving them information about college or other post-graduation options.**

A Broader Range of Obstacles

Work to College students with children differ significantly from childless students in their assessment of obstacles. Obstacles that parents cite as "significant" include credit card debt, nervousness

about academic requirements, lack of motivation or desire, low grades in high school, anxiety about SAT scores, society's attitude toward women in general, treatment of women in higher education, and a spouse or partner's lack of support.

Notably, this group is unique in its judgement that the "treatment of women in higher education" constitutes a significant obstacle: Returning students with children, specifically, in comparison with returning students overall, seem to judge college to be particularly unwelcoming or indifferent to their needs (13% of respondents with children cite this as a "significant obstacle," in comparison with 5% of respondents without children).

Children as Motivators

Women want to protect and provide for their children both in the short term, by providing the necessities, and in the long term, by financing their children's college education and other ambitions. Additionally, many women are motivated to go back to school to provide a positive role model for their children. Says a Los Angeles mom, "With the kids, you are going to

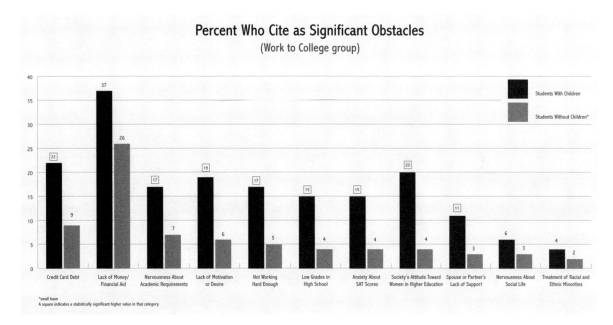

Percent Who Cite as Significant Obstacles
(Work to College group)

*small base
A square indicates a statistically significant higher value in that category.

> **"** *I have to finish school because of* **"**
> *my daughters. I'm their future.*
>
> —Los Angeles, Latina, high school senior

want to work more so you can support them. Most times, it's 'oh mommy, can I get this? Can I get that?'" An African American woman in Chicago comments, "There's another main reason why I want to [go to school] … for my daughter, because I want her to look at me and see what advantages it offers me [and] to know what advantages it will offer her."

Older women going back to school say they waited until their children were old enough or were out of the house before seeking additional education. Many of these women describe their return to school almost as a "selfish" act, or an act that fulfills their personal needs and wishes rather than those of their families.

Women in college with younger children, as revealed in focus groups, tended to be in more financially precarious situations and needed better-paying jobs more quickly to relieve financial burdens. As a Latina explains, "As soon as I got out of high school, I was pregnant, but as soon as I had my baby I got right back in … I'm not going to wait and not go to school, because this is the money I'm going to be supporting my family with. So I've got to rush on it." As primary caretakers of their families, women seek ways to coordinate their children's needs with their own. "What I had to worry about," says one low-income Altoona woman, "was finding time to study with two girls, and we did it together. They learned their ABCs while I was sitting at the table. They were at their level and I was at mine, but we still had family time."

EDUCATION AND PERCEPTIONS OF THE ECONOMY

■

How do women and men undergoing educational transitions envision the relationship between the economy, career, and education? Do they possess knowledge of job projections for the future and, if so, does this knowledge influence their education or work decision?

Particularly in the qualitative research, a few vivid, widely held perceptions of the interaction between education and the economy emerged. As confirmed in the quantitative research, there are some meaningful demographic differences in how men and women, whites and people of color, and older and younger students imagine the relationship between educational choices and the economy.

Does the Economy Matter in Educational Transitions?

A majority of those going to college say "yes." When asked if perceptions of future economic conditions and future job market projections influenced their decision to continue their education, 69 percent of the School to College group and 66 percent of the Work to College group respond affirmatively.

The percentage is reversed, however, for the School to Work group, where 63 percent report that the economy did not influence their decision not to go to college. Those who moved into the workforce directly out of high school may have faced exigencies that

prevented them from speculating on long-term career strategies, or they may be reporting that they are indifferent to economic considerations.

Rosy Views of Education and Career?

Notwithstanding the college-bound groups' conviction that they have factored economic considerations into their decision, other research points to a clash between career plans among high school students and economic projections. Olson notes that "Many students harbor career and college aspirations that bear little resemblance to reality." She writes, "the majority of high school students expect to become highly paid professionals, even though only about 20 percent of employment is in the professional ranks." Only one of every 60 high school graduates will become a doctor or a lawyer. "In contrast, only about six percent of high school seniors express a desire to become managers or technicians. Yet this is where the jobs are"—and will be in the next century. Schneider found much the same tension between goals and economic projections, noting that "the economy will not be able to accommodate the career choices of these young people. There won't be enough professional jobs. Girls believe that their chances of getting a well-paying job are as high as boys'. Blue collar jobs are not desired by either boys or girls. While young people can see themselves in professional roles, the likelihood of attaining such positions seems limited."[21]

Computers "Take Over"

All respondents—from both sexes and all ages, races, and ethnicities, and across all transition points—firmly believe that computers are, in a high school woman's words, "taking over the world."

Fully 85 percent of the Work to College and 78 percent of the School to College segments agree that "it is almost impossible to get a decent job today without a firm knowledge of computers." Seventy percent (70%) of the School to Work group feel that computer skills are "very important" to getting a good job today.

Significantly more women than men in the School to College group feel that "having computer skills" is "essential" to getting a good job (41% of women, 28% of men), although they may have interpreted "computer skills" to mean anything from word processing to advanced computer programming. Their assessment is borne out in estimates that 60 percent of new jobs by the year 2000 will require skills with information technologies. However, this certainty about the value of computer skills is not reflected in college women's choices of majors. In 1995 women received 28 percent of the computer and information sciences undergraduate degrees and only 10 percent of the engineering-related technologies degrees.[22]

In the focus group research, women elaborated their views of how computers are changing America's economy and increasing the pressure for ongoing education, knowledge, and training to keep up. Many describe the phenomenon in passive or resigned terms, as something that is inevitable, whether or not they feel equipped to meet its challenges. "Society is so focused on computers," a returning student comments, "I think there's going to be a big demand for that knowledge." A Los Angeles returning student

similarly predicts, "everything is going to be computers … you can't get around it," and a Chicago woman sees the need for "computer skills … everywhere, in everything." Women perceive that knowledge, especially around computer technology, is changing at a disorienting, rapid pace.

"The World is Getting Smarter and Smarter"

Almost unanimously, respondents undergoing any transition, and from all social backgrounds, feel that a high school degree and, to a lesser extent, a college degree, are essential for getting a job. Almost all of the School to College group say that a high school degree is "at least important" to getting a good job or advancing in a career, and 98 percent feel the same way about a college degree. Of that 98 percent, 38 percent of School to College students feel that the college degree is "essential" to getting a good job.

A similar percentage of the Work to College group—33 percent—deem a college degree essential for a good job. Among the School to Work group, 42 percent view the college degree as "very important," and 91 percent see it as at least "somewhat important."

The qualitative research revealed that many women feel that a bachelor's degree is almost "blasé," in one participant's terms, as the basic minimum requirement for securing a good career or job. These women imagine that educational demands for employment are steadily escalating and "getting higher and higher. You have to know more." Women will need to be "smarter and smarter" to keep up, so they will need to "get more education—more and more and more—because computers will probably be different and you're going to have to go back and learn something new again," as a Los Angeles woman predicts.

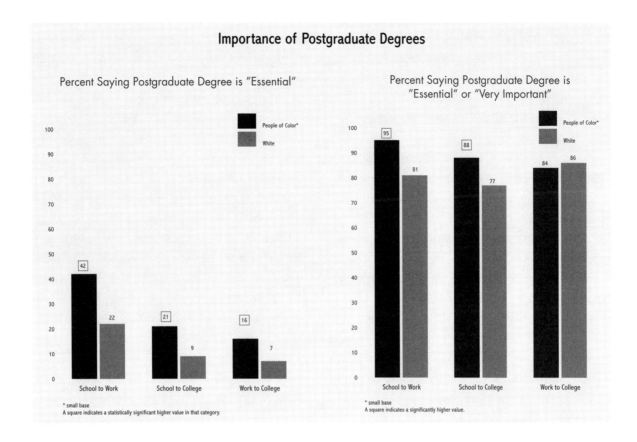

Importance of Postgraduate Degrees

Percent Saying Postgraduate Degree is "Essential"

- People of Color*
- White

	School to Work	School to College	Work to College
People of Color*	42	21	16
White	22	9	7

* small base
A square indicates a statistically significant higher value in that category.

Percent Saying Postgraduate Degree is "Essential" or "Very Important"

- People of Color*
- White

	School to Work	School to College	Work to College
People of Color*	95	88	84
White	81	77	86

* small base
A square indicates a significantly higher value.

Going Further/Getting Farther

Significantly more people of color than white survey respondents, across all three transition points, report that they think an advanced, postgraduate degree such as a master's is "essential" or "very important" for developing a promising career.

People of color report that a postgraduate degree is at least an "important" factor significantly more often than white respondents. They cite the degree as "essential" at a rate almost twice that of white respondents across all three transition groups. People of color believe more strongly in the value of an advanced degree or credential and feel that it will powerfully and positively affect their careers on the job market.

Ambivalence About the Value of Degrees

Although respondents are almost unanimous in their belief that a high school or, to a lesser extent, a college degree is a minimum prerequisite for success in the mercurial, knowledge-based economy of the 21st century, they reveal some ambivalence and contradictions about the value of a college education.

For example, there is a powerful dichotomy in people's minds between "real world" experience and educational credentials, despite widespread interest by educators and policy makers in re-imagining school and work as more fluid sites for learning. Focus group participants undergoing the Work to College transition, especially, identified social skills, experience, and networking "connections" as possible substitutes for the degree. As one puts it, "if you don't have connections, your butt is going back to school." Those with work experience, predictably, have a deeper appreciation for the amount of learning that occurs through work and greater skepticism about the applicability of classroom learning to careers.

The "Real World" or the "Piece of Paper"

The School to Work group rates interpersonal and "real world" experiences as somewhat more important in getting a good job than they do "getting good grades in college," "having a college degree," or "having a postgraduate degree." Ninety-one percent rank "having a college degree" as very or somewhat important, but all (100%) of the School to Work respondents rank "having people skills" as very or somewhat important.

Despite this positive assessment of a college degree, in another question 40 percent of the School to Work group agreed that "you don't need to go to college today to get a decent job."

In the two groups transitioning into college, a similarly ambivalent view of college and the job market emerges. Between 94 percent and 96 percent of the School to College and Work to College respondents agree that "in the future, it will be even harder to get a decent job without a college degree." However, only 33 percent of the Work to College and 38 percent of the School to College students see a bachelor's degree as "essential" to "getting a good job or advancing in a career."

As revealed in other responses, the **Work to College and School to College groups have surprisingly similar views of the relationship between education and the economy. A higher percentage of respondents rank "real world" experiences and people skills as "essential" to getting a good job than "having a college degree."** A high school degree receives the highest percentage of "essential" responses in each group, followed by people skills, critical thinking skills, real world workplace experience, interviewing skills, computer skills, and exposure to diverse ideas and cultures.

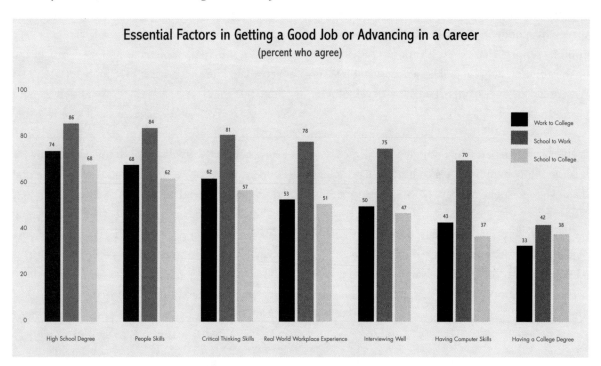

Essential Factors in Getting a Good Job or Advancing in a Career
(percent who agree)

When is Education Irrelevant?

Focus group participants returning to school echoed the opinion that these "real world" qualities and work experience are especially critical, and illustrated their points by contrasting the accretion of practical knowledge through work experience to "the piece of paper" or credential that higher education provides. Some women believed that for those who started their careers early and have worked steadily upward, education may be an expensive irrelevancy or diversion from their financial or personal advancement. A Chicago returning student explains, "it's not affecting my career at all … because of the age that I started work, and the consistency I've had in that career." An African American woman agrees that "what's going to progress me in my career is my work … . Your work is going to progress you farther than your schooling."

Educational Obsolescence?

Although women and men may occasionally deem education irrelevant to economic well-being, they see it as an actual detriment in only one or two cases. A few focus group participants noted that degrees and specific skills may be—or quickly become—obsolete, leaving college graduates with a "piece of paper" that cost thousands of dollars and creates few occupational opportunities. "Some people have credentials as long as your arm," a Work to College student cautions, "but [when] you talk to them, you discover that what they know just isn't applicable right now. It's not valuable." Another Chicago participant predicts that college graduates will need other experience to "substantiate that piece of paper, because I truly believe that it's going to be obsolete."

> "
> *With the downsizing thing today, you need to be careful about what you get your degree in … . There are a lot of degrees out there to get, and some don't matter anymore because things are getting so technical, limited, … and fixed.*"
>
> —Chicago, African American, Work to School

Solutions

Community Colleges—A Role Model?

■

Although community colleges have in the past been stereotyped as less rigorous than four-year institutions, **most students, including those in four-year colleges and universities, judge community colleges quite positively.** Not unexpectedly, the most favorable ratings of community colleges come from the Work to College group and students with children. Respondents praise community colleges for their institutional and curricular flexibility and for their responsiveness to nontraditional students, the most rapidly growing segment of postsecondary students.

Community colleges are seen as helpful in overcoming some of the obstacles that make it difficult for women, especially, to continue their education. As students in the School to College and Work to College groups explain, community colleges:

■ Offer a good deal financially
■ Offer more flexibility for students who have children or work
■ Provide additional academic assistance for those who need it
■ Provide practical and technical training
■ Provide quality instruction that is at least comparable to that of a four-year college.

About one-half to three-quarters of women in both of the college-bound groups agree with these positive statements about community colleges.

Mothers in the Work to College group are significantly more likely than women without

children to agree that community colleges are better for:

■ Students who work
■ Getting personal attention from faculty
■ First generation students
■ More practical training

Students in the Work to College group who are enrolled in two-year schools are significantly more likely than those who are enrolled in four-year schools to say that community colleges offer more personal attention from faculty and are better for students who work or have children.

> "
> *[Community college] is less expensive, closer to home, and right after high school I wasn't ready to go to a big university right away. I didn't know what I wanted to do. I wanted to go to a smaller college where I felt more comfortable just in preparation* "
> *for a university.*
>
> —Los Angeles, woman of color, transitioning from two-year to four-year college

Community College Strengths by Type of School Enrolled (percent who agree)	Work to College Group	
	Enrolled in four-year School	Enrolled in two-year School
Offer a better deal financially than four-year colleges or universities	75	78
Much better for below average students because they offer more academic assistance	74	78
Better for students with children	65	83
Better for students who work	61	75
Offer more practical and technical training	57	61
Offer more personal attention from faculty	51	70

A square indicates a statistically significant higher value in that category.

In addition to the schedule flexibility at community colleges and their convenient locations, focus group participants applauded the curricular flexibility at community colleges. They reported that it was easier to focus on career-related courses or courses of special interest to them, which expedites the completion process, and that for career areas where a four-year degree is not required, students can finish their courses and start a business faster. They found the two-year experience appropriate for students uncertain about their long-term educational goals. Finally, they underscored the more inviting atmosphere of a community college for students—particularly first-generation collegians—apprehensive about a large university setting. "I was scared because the [university] campus is big and … you have to be more responsible," a Los Angeles woman reports. "At a community college everything is minimized. Your responsibilities are minimized; the costs are minimized. There are not that many people, so you can adjust better. I got adjusted."

Community College Weaknesses

Along with these positive attributes, students say that community colleges have some significant deficiencies. A large percentage of students agree that community college students miss out on living away from home on a campus, which is in itself a valuable learning experience. Men are much more likely than women to say that community colleges are less academically rigorous than four-year institutions.

In addition, four in 10 women who are attending four-year schools in the School to College group and about two in 10 in the Work to College group would never consider going to a community college, despite their positive assessments of them.

Community colleges are important entry points for nontraditional and first-generation students, especially women. Their students value the schools' flexibility, accessibility, and support services.

MORE MONEY

■

More money for higher education and more financial aid options are critical in helping women to continue their education. **Women respondents in all three transition groups appear to be more influenced by financial restrictions, and more optimistic that financial incentives and aid will allow them to return to school (three-quarters of all women surveyed).** "More financial aid for anyone who needs it" is the item most often favored by women, significantly more than men in two of the three groups surveyed. Each of the groups also cite tax incentives to make it easier for people to continue their education as one of the top three needs. Across all three groups, two-thirds to over three-quarters of women favor more financial aid and tax incentives.

Among respondents in the School to Work group, more financial aid is especially important for those whose families had lower incomes at the time they graduated from high school.

Like the survey respondents, focus group participants would also like to see more financial aid, particularly in the form of scholarships and grants, rather than loans. "I am going to have to get some more

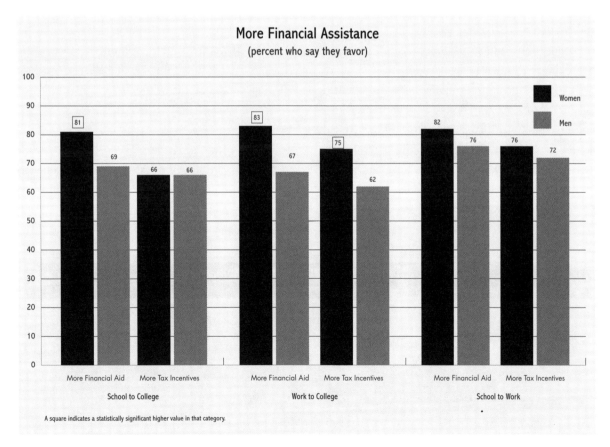

More Financial Assistance
(percent who say they favor)

A square indicates a statistically significant higher value in that category.

scholarships or something, because it is going to be too expensive for me," says one Latina teen. The idea of increasing their debt burden—as this report has shown, a more significant obstacle for women than for men—in order to attend schools, especially when many young women confess to already having debt, was an unacceptable trade-off for many of them. Other research has shown that work-study programs and off-campus employment tend to impede both the likelihood of college enrollment and completion rates for those students who do enroll. In one study, receipt of financial aid increased the probability of enrollment by 40 percent, but receipt of work-study depressed this increased probability.[23]

Again, as revealed especially in the qualitative research, flexibility is a key virtue in financial aid. Increasingly, students are finding that few can finish a degree in four years, and they want financial packages that are more realistic about the timing of education and supportive of "lifelong learning" and continuing education. The burgeoning population of older, nontraditional students may need funding for one or two classes, or for a certification program, rather than for a four-year (or longer) degree program that assumes full-time enrollment. Financial aid should no longer be designed solely according to the prototypical "college student" who is 18 years old and directly out of high school. Finally, many young people start school with high levels of debt and feel few programs take that fact into consideration or offer help.

Better Financial Aid Information

Not only would more money make a difference for all potential students, but so would more accessible and user-friendly information about money and financial aid. This is especially true for women, who are significantly more likely than men to cite "better information about financial aid" as an important factor in making education more accessible.

Focus group participants recommended, for example, meetings on how to apply for scholarships and a more proactive attitude from counselors and administrators, who, they emphasized, should volunteer information before students ask for it. Participants criticized the financial aid and grants process as byzantine, confusing, and inaccessible. "It is really a mess," summarizes a Baltimorean, "the people don't know what they are doing from one department to the next. It is ridiculous." Respondents trust that there are, indeed, sources of money "out there," but feel it requires great detective work— "digging" and "capturing"—to track them down. "Everyone always said there are scholarships out there, you've just got to look. And I'm not saying I looked, but they're at least very hard to find." According to the survey research, women experience the lack of a rational, user-friendly source of financial information and options as a particular barrier to higher education.

	School to College		Work to College		School to Work	
Better Financial Aid Information (percent who say they favor)	Women	Men	Women	Men	Women	Men
Better sources of information about financial aid	67	58	75	64	80	66

A square indicates a statistically significant higher value in that category.

Child Care and Support Services (percent who say they favor)						
	School to College		Work to College		School to Work	
	Women	Men	Women	Men	Women	Men
More services for students with special needs	61	44	65	48	57	55
College offering day care for students with children	58	37	74	57	67	50

A square indicates a statistically significant higher value in that category.

Child Care and Other Support Services

Providing affordable and convenient child care is another way to make college more accessible for women. In all groups, women are significantly more likely than men to say that day care offered by colleges would make going to college easier.

Women believe that juggling family, career, and education will pose even greater difficulties in the future, as women move more between work and education. Women are looking for more day care options, flexible scheduling, and courses at home through distance education. "They have to have on-campus child care. And if that is affordable, they will see a huge increase in women, young women, who are going back to school," a Chicago student argues.

Employer Incentives

Employers and coworkers lent encouragement to very few women in either the Work to College or the School to Work groups. Only about two in 10 said they were strongly encouraged by anyone at their workplace to return to school. **Nor did employers typically offer financial incentives for employees to pursue college. Yet those in the Work to College group who did receive financial incentives** overwhelmingly reported (75%) that it was an important factor in their return to school. While **employer assistance is relatively rare, then, they are highly effective motivators for women to continue their education.**

Women in the focus group recommended tax incentives to encourage employers to cover educational expenses and spoke highly of employers who permitted flexible work schedules.

Employer Encouragement and Nonmonetary Support

Employers are not key sources of encouragement for women in either the Work to College or the School to Work groups. In fact, bosses came in last in a list of possible motivators that included parents, teachers, friends, and coworkers. There is clearly room for improvement here, particularly because those respondents who did receive encouragement from their employers placed a great deal of importance on that support. Such support may take the form of flexible work schedules or job sharing to accommodate educational needs and schedules.

More Institutional Flexibility

Institutional flexibility, in terms of scheduling, core degree and major requirements, transfer of credits, class times, support services, and curricula, is a key to making college more accessible and feasible for all nontraditional Work to College students, but especially for women. From one-half to over three-quarters of women in all three groups favor support services and reforms that offer more flexibility to nontraditional students.

Seventy-six percent (76%) of the School to Work respondents overall report that "more flexible scheduling of classes" would have a significant impact on whether or not they would seek postsecondary education. Significantly more women than men in the Work to College group feel strongly that flexible scheduling of classes would make higher education more accessible (64% of women to 46% of men), which suggests that women feel especially constrained by the time demands of integrating a traditional college schedule into their lives. As a returning mother explains, "You have to figure out the class times … I had to go and see when I could take a class when [my son] was in school, so I didn't have to worry about all that."

"Pulling Together" a Degree

In focus groups, women spoke of difficulties in transferring credits from one institution to another, and fulfilling degree requirements for particular majors forestalled their completion of programs. They spoke, for example, of trying to "pull together" a bachelor's degree through a patchwork of previous college credits and current courses. "I have credits all over the place, and none of mine go together," comments an Altoona woman. Another reports that she took "the full length of time, six years," to complete a master's degree program because of the "sequencing of courses" and the logistical difficulties of obtaining certification. Sometimes a shift in majors means losing valuable time toward the completion of a degree, since a critical number of credits in the major have not been taken. Greater flexibility in transferring credits between institutions or programs within a college may help women coordinate their career, family, and educational goals.

Currently, the surge in "proprietary"-for-profit-postsecondary programs, which have grown from an obscure sector of the educational field to a $3.5 billion-a-year business, has been attributed to their success at offering flexible educational programs. Through convenient campus locations, classes that

More Flexibility						
	School to College		Work to College		School to Work	
	Women	Men	Women	Men	Women	Men
More flexible scheduling of classes to accommodate outside demands on students	55	44	69	53	79	72
More flexibility regarding the length of time needed to complete different programs	48	33	55	40	75	68

A square indicates a statistically significant higher value in that category.

run seven days a week and as late as 11:00 p.m., and comparatively reasonable tuition, proprietary postsecondary education appeals to nontraditional students.[24] Universities and colleges offer the advantage of a less technically or vocationally focused curriculum, but may lack the institutional and scheduling flexibility that make the proprietary programs attractive to the growing segment of nontraditional students.

Tangible Information

High school students facing a transition into the workforce or college report that more visits to college campuses and more and better information about career options would have been helpful. **Women survey respondents, in particular, favor information that comes from tangible, face-to-face contacts, mentors, and peer counselors**—for example, presentations by recent high school graduates or by representatives of various career paths, especially the more obscure ones. Among School to College women, nearly half feel that visits from recent college graduates and from college students were or would have been a "large help" in their decision-making process, in contrast to one-quarter of the School to College men. Substantially more Work to College women than men also feel that visits from college graduates would have been a large help to them as they made their transition.

Several focus group participants underscored the need for tangible sources of information about career and educational options. Otherwise, a Chicago woman recalls, "you know about it, but to know it and to actually experience it … or to know how to reach out and grasp it, is something different … . Nobody told me about golfing," she analogizes. "Golfing was if you had money … Nursing. You did not become a nurse. I was taught to be an LPN or a nurse's aide, not knowing that I could also be an RN." An African American woman elaborates, "The thing is that you have to relate to something. If I don't have any millionaires and doctors and lawyers in my immediate family, somebody that I can touch and talk to, then that's not something that I can achieve or I can have."

Although women have more interest than men in human contacts as sources of information, they are also more likely to consider a variety of sources of information influential, including books, their parents, teachers, counselors, and college visits.

Top Four Helpful Items When Planning for College (percent of women who thought item would be helpful)			
	School to College	Work to College	School to Work
More visits to college campuses	89	77	84
Recent college graduates visiting high schools to talk about their work experiences	86	84	82
College students visiting high schools to talk about their college experiences	86	81	85
More books and resources about college	83	80	82

Better Information about More Obscure Careers

With some consistency, participants in the focus groups recommended more information and resources in high school about obscure and unusual—but often rewarding and lucrative—career options. "You just hear about the main [choices] like a doctor, lawyer, and things like that. You don't hear about all those other little jobs that you can make a lot of money doing," a Latina suggests. An Altoona woman agrees: "You should have people come to your school and tell you about their careers, and not just the regular careers of lawyers, but other smaller things so you can get a feel for what they are interested in and talk to someone in the field."

Appendix

Demographic Profiles of Respondents
(by percent)

| | At the Time They Decided to Go to College | | | | When They Graduated High School | |
| | School to College | | Work to College | | School to Work | |
	Women	Men	Women	Men	Women	Men
Older than other students	7	5	32	31	10	23
Married	1	0	20	21	6	1
Pregnant/caring for a child	1	0	15	6	18	10
Recently divorced	0	0	6	3	0	0
Caring for a relative	1	0	5	3	8	6

The School to College and Work to College groups were asked if they experienced any of these life stages or events at the time they made the decision to continue their education.
The School to Work group was asked if they faced any of these life issues when they graduated from high school.

Endnotes

ENDNOTES

1. William Brody, "A University Campus in which Bits and Bytes Replace Bricks and Mortar," *Baltimore Sun,* February 26, 1997, p. 11A; U.S. Department of Education, "Building on What We've Learned: Developing Priorities for Education Research," May 24, 1996, p. 71; Donald Langenberg, "Diplomas and Degrees are Obsolescent," *Chronicle of Higher Education,* "Point of View," September 12, 1997; Julianne Basinger, "Former Michigan President Seeks to Turn Higher Education into a 'Knowledge Industry,'" Chronicle of Higher Education, website (www.chronicle.com), January 22, 1999; The National Collegiate Honors Council Forums, *Preparing for a Good Future: What Kind of Education Do We Need After High School?* (Englewood Cliffs, NJ: John Doble Research Associates, Inc., 1997), p. 2. See also Terry O'Banion, "A Learning College for the 21st Century," *Community College Journal,* 66, 1995–96 (December/January), pp. 18–23, which envisions a learning college that allows the learner to select options among prescribed modules, opportunities for collaboration with other learners, tutor-led groups, and other options.

2. Ernest Freeman and the Institute for Higher Education Policy, *Life After Forty: A New Portrait of Today's and Tomorrow's Postsecondary Students* (Washington, D.C.: Institute for Higher Education Policy, 1997); National Center for Postsecondary Improvement, *The Transition from Initial Education to Working Life in the United States of America* (Stanford, CA: NCPI, 1998), p. 6.

3. Additional Methodological Notes: Interviews lasted, on average, 24 minutes. At least four callbacks were made, staggered by day of week and time of day, to ensure that even the busiest respondents were reached. Follow-up appointments were scheduled with respondents who could not complete the interview when first contacted. Professional interviewers were utilized, with at least one supervisor always on hand. The sample was a mix of random digit dial (RDD) and, for students, the listed sample was obtained from American Student List. The listed sample was drawn to be as representative as possible, including students from all regions of the nation, public and private schools, and most competitive and least competitive schools.

4. Laura Rendon, "Access in a Democracy: Narrowing the Opportunity Gap" (unpub. Paper, National Postsecondary Education Cooperative, September 9, 1997), cited in Lawrence Gladieux and Watson Scott Swail, "Financial Aid is Not Enough," *The College Board Review,* Summer, 1998: pp. 3–11; *Reading and Mathematics Achievement: Growth in High School* (Washington, D.C.: U.S. Department of Education, National Center for Educational Statistics, 1997).

5. Educational Communications, *Who's Who Among American High School Students, 29th Annual Survey of High Achievers* (Lake Forest, IL.: ECI, 1998).

6. For example, 21.3% of female college students are 35 years or older, in comparison to 15% of male students. U.S. Department of Education, as reproduced in the *Chronicle of Higher Education Almanac, 1998–1999,* p. 18.

7. Educational Testing Service *Education for What? The New Office Economy* (Princeton: Educational Testing Service, 1998); on the "sub-baccalaureate labor market" see W. Norton Grubb, *Working in the Middle: Strengthening Education and Training for the Mid-Skilled Labor Force* (San Francisco: Jossey-Bass, 1996); "The South: All Shook Up," *The Economist,* September 19, 1998, p. 38.

8. Pennsylvania Commission for Women, *Financial Aid for Re-Entry Women Students: A Guide to Financial Resources* (Harrisburg, PA: Pennsylvania Commission for Women, 1994).

9. The Institute for Higher Education Policy, TERI, *Now What? Life After College for Recent Graduates* (Washington, D.C.: TERI, 1997), p. 7.

10. On the effect of stereotypes on learning and achievement, see Claude M. Steele, "Race and the Schooling of Black Americans," *Atlantic Monthly,* April 1992, pp. 68–78, and Steele, "Stereotype Threat and the Intellectual Test Performance of African Americans," *Journal of Personality and Social Psychology* 69, 1995: 797–811; and Margaret Shih, Todd Pitinsky, and Nalini Ambady, "Stereotype Susceptibility: Identity Salience and Shifts in Quantitative Performance," *Psychological Science* 10 (1), January, 1999, pp. 80–84.

11. A comprehensive 1997 study by researchers affiliated with the Educational Testing Service does note that the SAT underpredicts women's GPAs in college. However, the study cautions that grades, SAT scores, and other admissions variables when combined can provide a fairly accurate prediction of college achievement and bring "predicted and actual grades into optimal balance for some groups of students." Test scores "should not be used alone in academic prediction," the report notes. See Warren Willingham and Nancy Cole, *Gender and Fair Assessment* (Mahwah, NJ: Lawrence Erlbaum Associates, 1997), p. 310.

12. Bryan Mealer, "Moves Against Affirmative Action Fuel Opposition to Standardized Admissions Tests," *The Chronicle of Higher Education,* October 17, 1997.

13. The College Board, *Keeping the Options Open,* (New York: 1986); Millicent Lawton, "Split Personality: Pulled in Many Directions, High School Counselors Find Insufficient Time for Students' Academic Needs," *Education Week,* 29 April 1998, p. 31; Patricia McDonough, *Choosing Colleges: How Social Class and Schools Structure Opportunity* (Albany: SUNY Press, 1997).

14. A 1999 review of the state of high school counseling by Millicent Lawton includes, for example, the following account: A recent graduate of a well regarded magnet school in Washington recalls that her guidance counselor didn't even discuss college or the SAT college exam with students until it was almost too late—October of senior year. And even then, if a student sought her out individually, the woman reserved her time for those with high grade point averages or well-to-do families, ... Now a first year student at an Ivy League university, the young woman says that until the counselor calculated her GPA early in her senior year, the counselor had little time for her and advised her to look at less selective schools. But after the counselor learned the girl's grades put her in the top 10 students in the class, she suddenly became much more available and even tried to recruit the girl for a top liberal arts college in New England. While such treatment angered her then, the student figured out the counselor's logic: "Why waste all that information [on every member of the class] when she can focus on a few people that she thinks can get into a really good institution? It makes her look better. It's like a survival of the fittest type thing," the study says. "If she doesn't think highly of you, then she selects you out of it." See Millicent Lawton, "Split Personality," *Education Week.*

15. Lynn Olson, "When it Comes to Planning for Careers, High School Students Don't," *Teacher Magazine* 8 (1996); See also Olson, *The School to Work Revolution: How Employers and Educators are Joining Forces to Prepare Tomorrow's Skilled Workforce* (New York: Perseus Books, 1998).

16. Katherine Shaver, "For High School Students, A More Realistic Course," *Washington Post,* November 17, 1997, p. B1.

17. See Ernest Freeman and the Institute for Higher Education Policy, *Life After Forty: A New Portrait of Today's and Tomorrow's Postsecondary Students* (Washington, D.C.: Institute for Higher Education Policy, 1997).

18. Karen Arnold, *Lives of Promise: What Becomes of High School Valedictorians* (San Francisco: Jossey-Bass, 1995).

19. Jeffrey Breese, "Self Definition among Women Students," *Journal of Research and Development in Education* 29 (1995); Yenfang Tian, "Divorce, Gender Role, and Higher Education Expansion," *Higher Education* 32 (1), July, 1996, pp. 1–22.

20 M. Calloway, "A Model Program for Returning Women in Higher Education," *College Student Journal* 28 (September), 1994, pp. 281–86; J. King, "Single Parents: In Need of a Support Network," *Community College Journal* 65 (April, May), 1995, pp. 44–49.

21. Olson, *The School to Work Revolution,* p. 115; Barbara Schneider, "The Rising Tide of Ambitions Among Young Women," unpub. paper, AAUW Massachusetts, Spring Convention Symposium Proceedings, p. 6.

22. Figures from the U.S. Department of Education, as reproduced in the *Chronicle of Higher Education Almanac,* 1998–1999, p. 26.

23. Gay Young, "Chicana College Students on the Texas-Mexico Border: Tradition and Transformation," *Hispanic Journal of Behavioral Sciences* 14 (3), 1992, pp. 341–52; H. Cheng, "The Effects of Financial Aid on First Time College Attendance Decisions," paper presented at the Association for Institutional Research, 1997.

24. See Ben Gose, "Surge in Continuing Education Brings Profits for Universities," *Chronicle of Higher Education,* 19 February (1999). This article reports that proprietary, for-profit institutions have filled a need created by adult students where universities and colleges have failed to do so through their continuing education programs.

Researchers, Board, and Staff

Researchers

Jonathan Bick is a senior project manager at DYG, Inc. He has over five years of experience in the field of social science and market research. Bick graduated with distinction from the University of North Florida, and received his MA from the University of Connecticut.

Pamela Haag is the senior research associate at the AAUW Educational Foundation. She has researched and published extensively on gender and education, and on American cultural and women's history. She has a BA from Swarthmore College and her Ph.D. from Yale University.

Madelyn Hochstein is the president of DYG, Inc. and has over 25 years of experience in the field of social science and market research. She is well known in the field and regularly gives speeches on various public opinion topics. She is an elected member of the Market Research Council. Hochstein received a BA from Hunter College and an MA from the University of Pennsylvania.

Celinda Lake is president of Lake Snell Perry and Associates, and is a nationally recognized expert on political strategies, the women's vote and women's candidacies. Her most recent areas of concentration are the politics of the western states, children as a political issue, and the environmental movement today.

George Pettinico is the senior project manager at DYG, Inc., with several years of experience in the field of social science and market research. He has extensive expertise regarding study design, sampling, questionnaire composition, quantitative data analysis, and project management. Pettinico received his BA from Cornell University and MA from the University of Connecticut.

Victoria Sneed is an associate analyst at Lake Snell Perry and Associates. She has designed and analyzed survey research on a wide range of issues including children's health care, education, funding of alternative transportation, the environment, and the concerns of working women and families.

Selected Advisers and Readers

Professor Cheryl Bartholomew, George Mason University
Professor Sophia Catsambis, Queens College and CUNY Graduate Center
Professor Linda Williams, University of Maryland

Foundation Board and Staff

AAUW Educational Foundation Board of Directors

Maggie Ford, President
Lynne Aldrich, Development Vice President
Marion Kilson, Programs Vice President
Deborah Pavelka, Co-Finance Vice President
Wendy Shannon, Secretary
Eva Chess
Judith Horan
Gretchen Ilgenfritz
Loretta Jackson
Ruth Jurenko
Jean LaPointe
Jeanette Miller
Wendy Puriefoy
Elizabeth "Betty" Rawlins
Leila Shakkour
Florine Swanson
Sandy Bernard, AAUW President, Ex Officio

AAUW Educational Foundation Director

Karen Sloan Lebovich

AAUW Educational Foundation Project Staff

Priscilla Little, Research Director
Pamela Haag, Senior Research Associate

AAUW Equity Library

NEW!! Gaining a Foothold: Women's Transitions Through Work and College
Examines how and why women make changes in their lives through education. The report profiles three groups—women going from high school to college, from high school to work, and from work back to formal education—using both quantitative and qualitative methods. Findings include an analysis of women's educational decisionmaking, aspirations, and barriers. 100 pages/ 1999
$11.95 members/ $12.95 nonmembers

COMING THIS FALL!! Voices of a Generation: Teenage Girls on Sex, School, and Self
Compares the comments of more than 2,000 girls nationwide on peer pressure, sexuality, the media, and school. The girls were 1997 and 1998 participants in AAUW teen forums called Sister-to-Sister Summits. The report explores differences in girls' responses by race, ethnicity, and age, and offers the girls' platforms for action to solve common problems. For ordering information, visit AAUW's website at www.aauw.org.

Gender Gaps: Where Schools Still Fail Our Children
Measures schools' mixed progress toward gender equity and excellence since the 1992 publication of *How Schools Shortchange Girls*. Report compares student course enrollments, tests, grades, risks, and resiliency by race and class as well as gender. It finds some gains in girls' achievement, some areas where boys—not girls—lag, and some areas, like technology, where needs have not yet been addressed. 150 pages/1998.
$12.95 members/ $13.95 nonmembers.

Gender Gaps Executive Summary
Overview of *Gender Gaps* report with selected findings, tables, bibliography, and recommendations for educators and policymakers. 24 pages/1998.
$6.95 members/$7.95 nonmembers.

Separated By Sex: A Critical Look at Single-Sex Education for Girls
The foremost educational scholars on single-sex education in grades K-12 compare findings on whether girls learn better apart from boys. The report, including a literature review and a summary of a forum convened by the AAUW Educational Foundation, challenges the popular idea that single-sex education is better for girls than coeducation. 99 pages/1998.
$11.95 AAUW members/$12.95 nonmembers.

Gender and Race on the Campus and in the School: Beyond Affirmative Action Symposium Proceedings
A compilation of papers presented at AAUW's June 1997 college/university symposium in Anaheim, California. Symposium topics include: K-12 curricula and student achievement; positive gender and race awareness in elementary and secondary school; campus climate and multiculturalism; higher education student retention and success; and the nexus of race and gender in higher education curricula and classrooms. 1997.
$19.95 AAUW members/$21.95 nonmembers.

Girls in the Middle: Working to Succeed in School
Engaging study of middle school girls and the strategies they use to meet the challenges of adolescence. Report links girls' success to school reforms like team teaching and cooperative learning, especially where these are used to address gender issues. 128 pages/1996.
$12.95 AAUW members /$14.95 nonmembers.

Growing Smart: What's Working for Girls in School Executive Summary and Action Guide
Illustrated summary of academic report identifying themes and approaches that promote girls' achievement and healthy development. Based on review of more than 500 studies and reports. Includes action strategies, program resource list, and firsthand accounts of some program participants. 60 pages/1995.
$10.95 AAUW members/$12.95 nonmembers.

How Schools Shortchange Girls: The AAUW Report
Marlowe paperback edition, 1995. A startling examination of how girls are disadvantaged in America's schools, grades K–12. Includes recommendations for educators and policymakers as well as concrete strategies for change. 240 pages.
$11.95 AAUW members/$12.95 nonmembers.

Hostile Hallways: The AAUW Survey on Sexual Harassment in America's Schools
The first national study of sexual harassment in school, based on the experiences of 1,632 students in grades 8 through 11. Gender and ethnic/racial (African American, Hispanic, and white) data breakdowns included. Commissioned by the AAUW Educational Foundation and conducted by Louis Harris and Associates. 28 pages/1993.
$8.95 AAUW members/$11.95 nonmembers.

SchoolGirls: Young Women, Self-Esteem, and the Confidence Gap
Doubleday, 1994. Riveting book by journalist Peggy Orenstein in association with AAUW shows how girls in two racially and economically diverse California communities suffer the painful plunge in self-esteem documented in *Shortchanging Girls, Shortchanging America*. 384 pages/1994.
$15.00 AAUW members/$15.00 nonmembers.

Shortchanging Girls, Shortchanging America Executive Summary
Summary of the 1991 poll that assesses self-esteem, educational experiences, and career aspirations of girls and boys ages 9-15. Revised edition reviews poll's impact, offers action strategies, and highlights survey results with charts and graphs. 20 pages/1994.
$8.95 AAUW members/$11.95 nonmembers.

Order Form

Name _____

Address _____

City/State/ZIP _____

Daytime phone (_____) _____

AAUW membership # (if applicable) _____

Item	Circle Price Member/Nonmember	Quantity	Total
Gaining a Foothold	$11.95/$12.95	_____	_____
Gender Gaps: Where Schools Still Fail Our Children	$12.95/$13.95	_____	_____
Gender Gaps Executive Summary	$6.95/$7.95	_____	_____
Separated By Sex	$11.95/$12.95	_____	_____
Gender and Race on the Campus and in the School	$19.95/$21.95	_____	_____
Girls in the Middle: Working to Succeed in School	$12.95/$14.95	_____	_____
Growing Smart Executive Summary and Action Guide	$10.95/$12.95	_____	_____
How Schools Shortchange Girls	$11.95/$12.95	_____	_____
Hostile Hallways	$8.95/$11.95	_____	_____
SchoolGirls	$15.00/$15.00	_____	_____
Shortchanging Girls Executive Summary	$8.95/$11.95	_____	_____
	Subtotal:		_____
	Sales Tax (DC, MD residents only):		_____
	International Order Surcharge (25% of subtotal above):		_____
	Shipping/Handling (see chart below):		_____
AAUW Membership-at-Large	$40	_____	_____
	Total Order:		_____

For bulk pricing on orders of 10 or more, call 800/225-9998 ext. 503.

Please make check or money order payable in U.S. currency to AAUW. Do not send cash.

AAUW Federal Identification Number 53-0025390

Credit cards are accepted for orders of $10 or more.

❏ MasterCard ❏ Visa   Card #__ __ __ __ - __ __ __ __ - __ __ __ __ - __ __ __ __ Expiration _____

Name on card _____

Cardholder signature _____

SATISFACTION GUARANTEED: If you are not completely satisfied with your purchase, please return it within 90 days for exchange, credit, or refund. Videos are returnable only if defective, and for replacement only.

❏ Please send me information on joining an AAUW branch in my area (dues vary by branch).

❏ I'd like to join as a member-at-large. Enclosed is $40. (Fill in education information below.)

_____ _____ _____
College/University   State/Campus   Year/Degree

Shipping and Handling	
Up to $10	$3
$10.01–$50	$5
$50.01–$75	$7
$75.01–$100	$9
$100.01–$300	$12
Over $300	5% of subtotal

FOR MAIL ORDERS, SEND THIS FORM TO:
AAUW Sales Office
Dept. 503
P.O. Box 251
Annapolis Junction, MD 20701-0251

FOR TELEPHONE ORDERS, CALL:
800/225-9998 ext. 503
301/206-9789 fax

CODE: M00MFE